ETSY 101

Sell Your Crafts on Etsy, the DIY Marketplace for Handmade, Vintage and Crafting Supplies

www.Etsy101.com

By Steve Weber
with Laurie Jackson
Editor: Julie Bird

Published by Stephen W. Weber
Printed in the United States of America
Weber Books   www.WeberBooks.com
ISBN: 9781936560097

Also by Steve Weber:

The Home-Based Bookstore: Start Your Own Business Selling Used Books on Amazon, eBay or Your Own Web Site

Sell on Amazon: A Guide to Amazon's Marketplace, Seller Central, and Fulfillment by Amazon Programs

eBay 101: Selling on eBay For Part-time or Full-time Income, Beginner to PowerSeller in 90 Days

Barcode Booty: How I found and sold $2 million of 'junk' on eBay and Amazon, and you can, too, using your phone

Plug Your Book! Online Book Marketing for Authors, Book Publicity through Social Networking

www.Facebook.com/Etsy101

www.Etsy101.com

Contents

ACKNOWLEDGMENTS

I'm indebted to everyone who graciously donated their time and expertise to contribute ideas, examples, photographs, corrections, clarifications and other improvements to this book:

Angie Barrett	Suds 'N Such
Elizabeth Cogliati	Lizbeth's Garden
W.J. Elvin III	Villa de la Lega
Rebecca George	Purple and Lime
Georgianne Holland	Nestle And Soar
Laurie Jackson	Indulge Your Shelf
Josie Marsh	Wooly Baby
Stephanie Maslow	Metalicious
Jessica Partain	Inedible Jewelry
Susan Partain	Inedible Jewelry
Susannah Rain-Haddad	Zou Zou's Basement
Jennifer Schmidt	Jenna's Red Rhino
Rachel Steck	Custom Hemp Treasures
Cathy Stein	Eclectic Skeptic

Also, I'm grateful for the hard work of my editor, Julie Bird, who sweeps up after my countless errors, and my collaborator Laurie Jackson, who swiftly kicked the tires on this book's draft, contributing dozens of corrections, clarifications and new ideas.

—Steve Weber

INTRODUCTION

A few years ago, when Joe and Amy Sharp of Columbus, Ohio, had their first child, they were alarmed by frequent safety recalls of the boy's plastic toys, all mass-produced in China.

Of course, what parent wouldn't worry about a baby teether contaminated with lead?

But unlike most parents, Joe, a carpenter, decided to chuck the plastic toys and replace them, one by one, with simple hand-cut wooden blocks and rattles he made at home. To his surprise, his son enjoyed the plain wooden toys just as much as the colorful plastic ones he'd thrown out. And since Joe made his toys with local wood, he knew they were safe. When friends began asking for some of the toys, Joe and Amy put their heads together and decided to turn the family's new hobby into cash.

Having a good idea is one thing, but making it pay off is another. The Sharps knew that starting a business is a crapshoot, even in the best of times. Opening a toy store would require a huge cash outlay. Selling at craft fairs would require lots of time and travel. Starting a website to sell toys seemed complicated and risky, too.

So in 2007, Joe and Amy settled on opening a storefront on Etsy.com, a new Internet shopping mall for crafts and collectibles. Within two years, their Etsy shop, "Little Alouette," was their main source of income. They needed employees to help mail the orders, had recruited six retail distributors, and launched a website for wholesale orders. And they were just getting started.

Joe and Amy had stumbled onto a white-hot business trend: selling handcrafted items online that shoppers can't find in a regular store. Thousands of Etsy crafters, young and old, have done the same, launching their business on a shoestring, usually part-time at home. Often the whole business—crafting, product photography, customer service, and order fulfillment—is done by the artisans themselves—knitters, painters, weavers, soap-makers, cupcake bakers, hobbyists and fashionistas of every stripe. Customers discover the goodies through old-fashioned word of mouth, amplified and accelerated by online social networks such as blogs, Facebook, Twitter, and search tools at Google and Etsy itself.

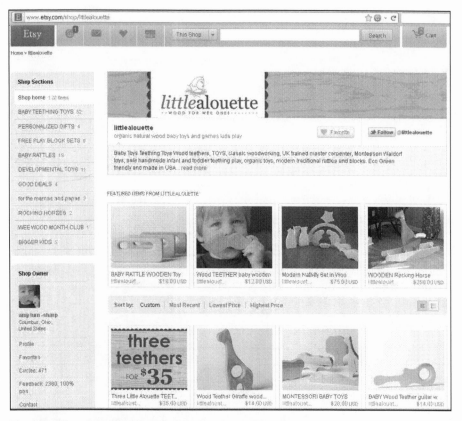

The Etsy shop for Little Alouette handmade wooden toys.

The buzz has thousands of new buyers flocking to Etsy.com daily, shopping for one-of-a-kind gifts and goodies for every conceivable taste and occasion—top hats, handmade mittens, little black dresses, vanilla shampoo, and earrings that look like a tiny slice of key-lime pie (or other favorite desserts). And just in case you don't find anything you want among the 12 million items on sale at any given moment, you can place a custom order and get your exact wish, made from scratch.

For crafters, it's a revolution. Never before has it been possible (actually, Etsy makes it fairly easy) to open a worldwide business with millions of paying customers, with virtually no up-front investment, all in an afternoon.

Sound too good to be true? If you're a skilled crafter or artist, you're 90 percent home free. Honing your crafting chops—and mustering up the courage to sell your creations, is the hard part.

By contrast, the techniques covered in this book (registering at Etsy and learning to photograph, list and promote your items) are relatively easy—but just as important to your success.

There are no secrets in this book, but I hope you'll find it a useful roadmap for your creative, entrepreneurial adventure, helping you avoid some blind alleys, and having a chuckle here and there.

We'll start things off simple. We'll do some dreaming, get into some nitty-gritty, and boil it down again. Essentially, it's a philosophy I've developed as an online merchant myself, and by picking the brains of the Etsy sellers featured in these pages: Just sell what you know and love, obsess about making your customers happy, and give everyone the benefit of the doubt. Everything flows from that.

A footnote on safety and children's products

After widely publicized safety recalls of mass-produced toys, Congress mandated testing and labeling with the 2008 Consumer Product Safety Improvement Act, or CPSIA. In 2011, recognizing the law's burden on crafters, Congress provided relief. Sellers with less than $1 million in annual sales will be exempted from expensive third-party testing.

More details are posted here: Cpsc.gov/about/cpsia/cpsia.html.

How we got here

Not long ago, most crafters struggled to earn a living. Potters, knitters, woodworkers, and artists spent years learning their craft, and many of them never had much chance to show off their creations, let alone sell much. They'd put some on a wagon, stuff it in a backpack, or throw it in a pickup truck or station wagon. They might blow their last two dollars on gasoline to lug their wares to a craft show in the next county. Often, it was a waste of time, with not a single sale. Sure, you might meet some decent folks and chat away a Saturday afternoon. But then you'd have to pack it all back up, and haul it back on a drive home that seemed twice as long as the drive there. No matter how good you were, everybody was limited by geography. And if you lived in the sticks ... well, you spent a lot of time whittling.

It wasn't any easier for dealers of antiques and other curiosities who toiled away in antique malls, flea markets, and broken-down shops dotting rural highways. You spent a wad on a storefront, rent and utilities, insurance, and employees—and lost a bundle before you earned a single dollar.

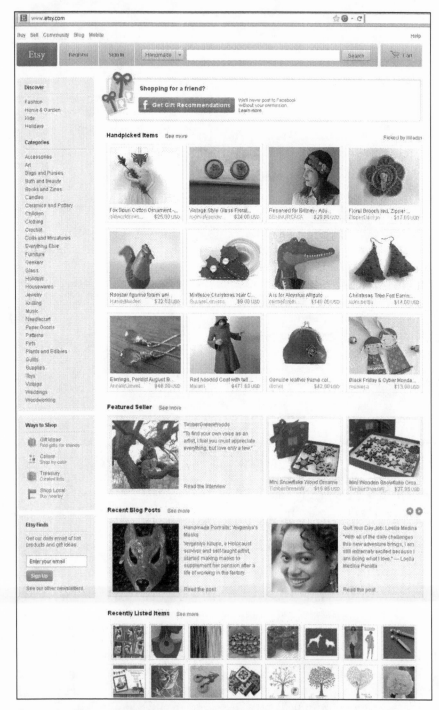

Etsy.com offers a world of buying and selling opportunities.

However you tried it, crafting and selling unique creations was hard. And the harder you worked, the more money you paid to a long line of middle-men.

Now, for a change, you can depend on yourself. Etsy is a godsend for craf-ters who haven't had easy access to craft shows, for whom travel is difficult, or those folks without the smooth-talking flair of a carnival barker. Using an Internet storefront, you can sell more items more quickly, earn more money, and have more fun, spending more of your time doing what you loved in the first place—making new stuff, finding new treasures, and meeting lots of new people obsessed with the same stuff as you. Even if you're shy.

Etsy (the name rhymes with "Betsy," and means "oh, yes!" in Italian), in just a few years, has become the world's marketplace for handmade and vintage items. It's growing like a beanstalk in a tub of Miracle-Gro right under the sun, racking up a billion dollars in sales during its short lifetime, and growing by double-digit percentages every few months.

The genius of Etsy

Etsy was started in 2005 by Rob Kalin, an artist and carpenter who was look-ing for a place to sell his work online. At the time, one of the few alternatives was eBay, but it wasn't a good fit for crafters and artists. Even more so today, eBay has a decided bargain-bin flavor, often featuring big sellers of mass-produced seen-on-TV junk and Chinese knockoffs.

Kalin gathered some of his computer-whiz friends from college, and they cobbled together Etsy's site. It wasn't your dad's eBay; Etsy was conceived from the start as a platform enabling individual artisans to sell what they made, directly to buyers. And that's exactly what makes Etsy tick—it encour-ages direct communication between the artisan-merchant and the customer, a practice virtually outlawed now at corporate websites like eBay and Ama-zon, and often lacking at local full-service retailers, too.

So even though he invented it, Rob Kalin isn't the genius of Etsy. No, the brains behind Etsy is the collective wisdom, wants, and joy of its millions of users. It adds up to an electric, addictive social shopping experience, unlike anything possible before. It's like "real" shopping, but faster, friendlier, unique, and without most of the hassles that plague an actual shopping trip—parking tickets, traffic jams, waiting at the checkout, lugging it home....

Etsy founder Rob Kalin

Oh sure, just like real shopping, on Etsy you might accidentally max out your credit card. But you won't have to worry about whether you've got enough cash left to get home. Plus, after you start selling your own stuff on Etsy, you'll be able to afford lots more shopping!

Despite Etsy's tight focus, it has spawned a constantly expanding universe of unique creations and keepsakes—art, photography, jewelry, homemade candy, clothing, handmade soaps and lotions, toys. And that's just the hand-made stuff—there's also "vintage" items, like the collectors' items that used to haunt eBay (old snowshoes, wooden wagons, shotgun shells strung together as a necklace) and every imaginable crafting supply—beads, patterns, buttons, yarn, sparkly things. Your imagination is the only limit.

Etsy's theme is an old-fashioned craft fair, where each seller has their own booth for selling their stuff. But unlike a "real" craft fair, Etsy is open every day of the year, not just a few weekends. There are no travel costs, and the rent is absurdly low—20 cents for each item you list. When it sells, you pay Etsy a commission of 3.5 percent, and a fee to PayPal, if you use it to process your online payments.

Looking for gifts that your friends and family actually want? Here are handmade Etsy items that pop up based on the interests of my Facebook friends. They'll think you shopped all week! (See instructions in the chapter, "Mine the Etsy Community.")

Etsy's success is the perfect storm of an overflowing pool of online shoppers, a swelling population of business-savvy crafters, and burgeoning demand for unique handmade goods from people weary of cookie-cutter clothing and furnishings shipped from overseas sweatshops.

Etsy is riding the wave toward sustainable living, a do-it-yourself culture, and a backlash against robotic consumerism and consumption—not only in the United States, but across the developed world. In the 1980s and '90s, big name brands were king. It was cool to be "preppy" and have a tiny alligator— or a big corporation's name—emblazoned across your shirt. Now, not so much. People want something little, something special, something worth coveting and treasuring. Perhaps something made especially for them, simple or frilly, from an artist or designer they personally admire and feel connected with.

Exactly who is doing all the heavy lifting here? It's impossible to stereotype, but Etsy's executives say the site's membership is overwhelmingly female, on both the buying side and selling side. Many are college-educated women in their twenties and thirties. Some are stay-at-

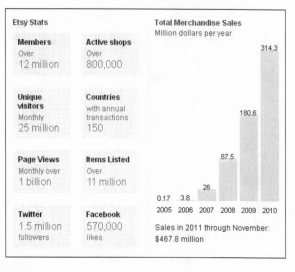

home moms who aren't yet ready for full-time employment, but have a hand-crafting skill they'd enjoy turning into some cash—and perhaps building into a full-time venture later. And, of course, plenty of Etsians are veteran crafters who are gladly leaving the craft-show circuit behind for a more easygoing, profitable alternative. Another cohort of Etsy folk are those with full-time jobs who enjoy crafting on evenings and weekends for extra cash, perhaps with an eye toward quitting the day job, and working just for themselves some day. And if there's one thing I've learned from having my own business, it's this: working hard for yourself is a lot easier than hardly working for someone else.

According to recent figures from Etsy's staff, the average transaction is about $17, including the crafting supplies sold on the site. There are more buyers than sellers (that's a good thing, if you're selling). Altogether about 200,000 Etsy sellers rack up more than $50 million in sales a year to the site's 16 million registered customers.

What's allowed on Etsy

You can offer three main types of merchandise for sale on Etsy:

- **Handmade by you.** Created by the seller or a member of a collective Etsy shop.

- **Crafting supplies.** Includes handmade and commercial items used to make handmade items.

- **Vintage goods.** Items at least 20 years old.

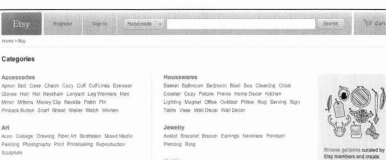

Etsy | Register | Sign In | Handmade ▾ | [   ] | Search | ☒ Cart

Home > Buy

Categories

Accessories
Apron Belt Case Charm Cozy Cuff Cuff Links Eyewear
Gloves Hair Hat Keychain Lanyard Leg Warmers Men
Mirror Mittens Money Clip Necktie Patch Pin
Pinback Button Scarf Shawl Wallet Watch Women

Art
Aceo Collage Drawing Fiber Art Illustration Mixed Media
Painting Photography Print Printmaking Reproduction
Sculpture

Bags and Purses
Backpack Clutch Diaper Bag Hip Bag Laptop Messenger
Novelty Pouch Purse Tote Wallet Wristlet

Bath and Beauty
Bath Body Fragrance Hair Lip Balm Lotion Makeup Men
Oil Salve Scrub Skin Care Soap

Books and Zines
Album Book Bookmark Comic Journal Zine

Candles
Beeswax Container Holder Incense Pillar Scented
Shaped Soy Taper Tart Tea Light Tin Travel Unscented
Vegan Votive

Ceramics and Pottery
Bowl Coaster Cup Decoration Home Decor Jar Jewelry
Kitchen Miniature Planter Plate Pot Sculpture Serving
Soap Dish Supplies Teapot Tile Vase

Children
Accessories Art Baby Bath Clothing Furniture
Housewares Jewelry Toddler Toy

Clothing
Children Corset Costume Dress Hoodie Jacket Lingerie
Maternity Men Pants Plus Size Shawl Shirt Shoes Shorts
Skirt Sleepwear Socks Sweater Sweatshirt Swimsuit Tank
Tshirt Underwear Vest Women

Crochet
Accessories Afghan Bags and Purses Clothing Cozy Doll
Hat Housewares Jewelry Scarf Supplies

Dolls and Miniatures
Amigurumi Animals Art Doll Artist Bears Child Friendly
Fantasy Fashion Dolls Apparel Figurines Human Figure Doll
Miniature Plush Primitive Puppets Reborns
Scale Dollhouse Miniature Scale Models Soft Sculpture
Waldorf

Everything Else
Custom Educational Graphic Design Magic Metaphysical
Personalized Pocket Religious Taxidermy Weird

Furniture
Bed Bench Bookcase Chair Desk Dresser Entertainment
Fixture Mirror Shelf Storage Table

Geekery
Accessory Clothing Computer Electronic Fantasy Gadget
Horror Housewares Humor Jewelry Kitsch Magic Robot
Science Toy Videogame Weird

Glass
Bead Bottle Bowl Cabochon Coaster Dish Glassware
Home Decor Jewelry Magnet Marbles Mirror Ornament
Paperweight Pipe Sculpture Stained Glass Suncatcher
Supplies Vase Windchime

Holidays
Birthday Christmas Day of the Dead Easter Halloween
Hanukkah New Years Patriotic St Patricks Thanksgiving
Valentine

Housewares
Basket Bathroom Bedroom Bowl Box Cleaning Clock
Coaster Cozy Fixture Frame Home Decor Kitchen
Lighting Magnet Office Outdoor Pillow Rug Serving Sign
Table Vase Wall Decal Wall Decor

Jewelry
Anklet Bracelet Brooch Earrings Necklace Pendant
Piercing Ring

Knitting
Accessories Baby Bags and Purses Blanket Children
Clothing Cozy Doll Hat Housewares Jewelry
Knitting Supplies Men Scarf Sweater Women

Music
Case Cd Equipment Instrument Mp3 Poster Strap Tape
Video Vinyl

Needlecraft
Accessories Clothing Cross Stitch Doll Embroidery Felted
Holidays Jewelry Needlepoint Pattern Pillow Pincushion
Supplies

Paper Goods
Bookmark Bookplate Calendar Cards Gift Wrap Journal
Notebook Origami Pad Papermaking Scrapbooking
Stationery Sticker Tag

Patterns
Accessories Amigurumi Baby Beading Clothing Crochet
Cross Stitch Doll Clothing Embroidery Handmade Holiday
Home Knitting Painting Plushie Quilt Sewing

Pets
Accessories Bag Bed Blanket Bowl Carrier Clothing
Collar Feeding Grooming Harness House Leash
Pet Lover Pillow Portrait Small Animal Tag Toy Treat

Plants and Edibles
Baked Goods Candy Coffee Dried Herb Jam Marmalade
Plant Recipes Sauce Snack Spice Tea Vegan

Quilts
Applique Baby Bed Crazy Fabric Postcard Geometric Mini
Patch Patchwork Pillow Rag Table Runner Traditional
Trim Wall Hanging

Supplies
Bead Button Cabochon Commercial Fabric Handmade
Knitting Pattern Scrapbooking Yarn

Toys
Amigurumi Baby Bear Blythe Children Doll Doll Clothes
Food Game Miniature Plush Pretend Puppet Puzzle
Sports Waldorf

Vintage
Accessories Antique Bags and Purses Book Clothing
Collectibles Electronics Furniture Home Decor Housewares
Jewelry Paper Ephemera Serving Supplies Toy

Weddings
Accessories Album Bags and Purses Basket Bouquet
Cake Topper Candle Card Clothing Decoration Favor
Frame Guest Book Invitation Jewelry Just Married Men
Pillow Portrait Something Blue

Woodworking
Accessories Bowl Box Burning Carving Clock Fretwork
Furniture Home Decor Housewares Inlay Jewelry Kitchen
Miniature Office Outdoor Sculpture Seasonal Sign Sport
Supplies Toy

Browse galleries curated by Etsy members and create your own.

Explore Treasury

We've got personalized suggestions for everyone on your list.

Find Gifts

Prohibited on Etsy

Etsy doesn't allow resellers. In other words, you can't sell items made by another crafter (except for a few special cases we'll discuss later). Neither may you sell mass-produced items that appear handmade (although non-handmade items are allowed in the Vintage and Supplies categories). Other prohibited items are alcohol, drugs, animals, firearms, weapons, pornography, tobacco, motor vehicles, real estate, and recalled items.

OK, you've got the main idea. Now we'll get into some details.

SELLER PROFILE: Inedible Jewelry

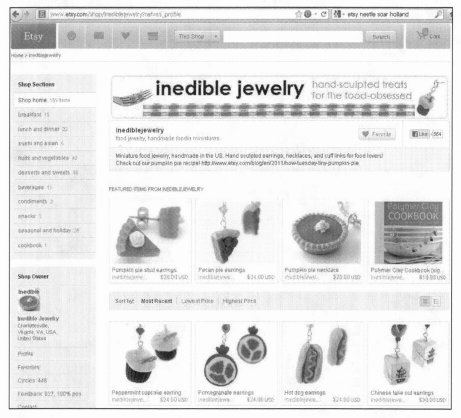

Inedible Jewelry of Charlottesville, Va., serves up handmade food-themed jewelry including earrings, necklaces, and cufflinks in the shape of just about everyone's favorite foods—hot dogs, cupcakes, a piece of pumpkin pie. Sisters Jessica and Susan Partain began sculpting and baking these tiny treats made from polymer clay as a fun hobby, but it has mushroomed into big business.

See **Etsy.com/shop/inediblejewelry**.

How did you get started?

We began sculpting miniature food when we were kids, about 20 years ago. We started out creating dollhouse foods, then decided they'd be more fun as jewelry for people to wear, instead of static miniatures.

Jessica and Susan Partain greet customers at a craft show in Washington, D.C.

In 2006, we started selling our work at local markets in Charlottesville, Va., and the business grew from there. In 2007, we launched our Etsy shop as an adjunct to our stand-alone website. Now we redirect all our visitors to Etsy.

How has your business evolved and weathered the economy?

At first, we wanted an outlet for our hobby. The first week we sold at our market, we made sales, and had a great response. In a few months, we expanded from a single table to three tables with large vertical displays and a bigger line. I was in graduate school, and Susan had a full-time job at a nonprofit. Within six months, I had decided to go full time, and Susan still works part time on Inedible Jewelry. Now we sell weekly at markets and shows for nine months of the year. And we have several wholesale accounts, including the Smithsonian's National Museum of American History gift shop.

We've managed the economic downturn because we offer something fun and unique. We fill a niche market, catering to the whimsical side of accessories.

Where do you get new ideas?

We're both food-obsessed, so our creative process really boils down to investigating new foods. We're constantly brainstorming fun new designs. Our major limiting factor now is balancing our proven best-sellers with new designs. We read food blogs, chat with foodies on Twitter, cook real foods, and ask our customers what they want.

How do you find customers and repeat business?

Targeted marketing brings in customers. Our customers appreciate handmade work, food, and they're playful. We're on Facebook and Twitter, and constantly networking with people who share similar interests. Everyone loves food, and playful people also like to wear their favorite foods!

We get repeat business by concentrating on great customer service, providing a fantastic quality product, and generally being upbeat and fun.

How big is your online business compared with shows and markets?

About a third of our business is shows and markets, about a third is online, and the other third is wholesale clients.

How do you price your items?

We base our pricing on labor, materials, and overhead—keeping wholesale in mind. We keep highly detailed records of how long it takes to make our pieces, and our exact costs of materials and overhead. We want to price each piece correctly, so we reevaluate pricing quarterly. Because we sell retail and wholesale, we ensure we're paid for our time creating the pieces, and marketing and selling, which is time-consuming, too.

Can you give advice about paid advertising?

I honestly can't give direct advice because we've never paid for advertising. Online, our approach has focused on word of mouth—Facebook and Twitter have been huge assets—and carefully selected collaborations with other websites. We collaborate with high-profile blogs that target our market, but from a different angle. And we work hard on keywords and Search Engine Optimization.

We've done some fun giveaways with foodie blogs, and that's gotten our name out there without advertising. Also, I'm preparing to teach a class on making tiny pumpkin pies at Etsy Labs in New York. It will be great personal publicity there, and promoted on Etsy's home page for at least three days. It will drastically raise our profile and bring in lots of traffic.

www.etsy.com/listing/64943494/valentines-cupcake-necklace

Valentines cupcake necklace

This sweet handmade cupcake necklace is the perfect accessory for your favorite Valentine!
A tiny inedible vanilla cupcake with pink buttercream frosting and a teensy red heart- what
could better say "I love you?"

For crafters just getting started, I recommend spending some serious time figuring out your target market and learning Google Analytics. Before paying for any advertising, it's essential to understand where your traffic is coming from, and measuring your success with keywords. Without some baseline, it's impossible to know whether your advertising is effective or a waste of money.

You wrote a wonderful book describing your crafting techniques, *The Polymer Clay Cookbook*. Did you worry about giving away your secrets and creating competition for your jewelry?

I believe in sharing what you've learned. I am mostly self-taught, but I love to teach classes in sculpting polymer clay, and have been doing it since 2007.

We knew people would copy the designs in the book and sell them. But we weren't too worried. We're constantly inventing new designs and pushing our sculpting skills to new levels. So we'll always have something new. And if we inspire other crafters, that's fantastic.

Two kinds of people like our work—those who want to purchase it, and those who want to make it themselves. By offering our finished pieces—along with a how-to book—we provide something for everyone. Also, the book is an elegant response to those inevitable folk who question our pricing, or say, "Oh, I can make that myself." We just smile and say, "Absolutely!" People who try it have a much deeper appreciation for our work afterwards.

REGISTER AND SHOP AT ETSY

We're starting at square one: registering at Etsy, and going shopping. If you're already an Etsy member, you can skim through this chapter, and use it as a review of the buying process. But if you're new to Etsy, don't skip this part. Our objective is to be a great Etsy seller, and the first step is becoming intimately familiar with the buying process.

Registration is easy at Etsy.com, using your Facebook account or your email address.

Registering at Etsy is easy. At Etsy.com, click the Register link near the top right. Fill in the form, and Etsy will send a confirmation e-mail. Click the link in the confirmation email Etsy sends to certify you're the owner of your email address.

When registering, you'll select a user name of up to 20 characters—letters and numbers only, no spaces or symbols. For now, you can use a placeholder user name. Later, when you've firmly decided on a business name, you can edit your Etsy user name to match it.

Your Etsy avatar. You can upload a digital "profile picture," and a small square version will appear with your user name on Etsy—with your profile, and where you post on Etsy message boards. For their avatar, some people use a portrait of themselves, a photo of a favorite item, or a logo. To upload your avatar, go to Your Account > Profile. Click the Browse button and select the image file from your computer. Etsy will convert the image to a square image, 75 pixels by 75 pixels. So if the picture you upload isn't square, it might appear distorted, or be cropped at the sides.

 Some occasional Etsy users might not bother uploading an avatar at all. In that case, they're represented on Etsy with a default silhouette shown at left. Having the perfect avatar will be important later, when we explore selling.

As with all content you post to Etsy, your avatar must be your property—a photo or design you've prepared yourself, or obtained permission to use. Violating copyright laws or infringing on another's intellectual property is verboten at Etsy. We'll examine this in detail later; for now, suffice to say you can't use something that isn't yours on Etsy.

If you need to modify an existing photo for use on Etsy, you can use image software such as Adobe Photoshop, or one of the several free tools we'll explore in the chapter "Create and Edit Your Listings."

Draw your privacy boundaries

Etsy allows members to limit access to two items regarding your account—your user name, and your email address.

For example, Etsy members can discover your email address if it's publicly displayed on Etsy. However, you can change this default setting by pressing the "no" button in Your Account > Privacy Settings. Selecting "No" also means that your Etsy user name won't appear when other members import their contact lists to Etsy. Likewise, you can change the default setting for your Favorites by clicking private instead of public.

In your account settings, you can limit access to your user name and email address.

It's understandable that a casual Etsy buyer might prefer keeping their email address private. On the other hand, as a seller you'll probably want to make it as easy as possible for shoppers to reach you.

For more details on how Etsy handles personal information, review Etsy's Privacy Policy at Etsy.com/policy/privacy. Another important policy is Etsy's Terms of Use at Etsy.com/help/article/479.

Set your reach with 'region preference'

As an Etsy shopper, you can indicate a "region preference" to ensure that your search results include only those items available for shipping to your location. Certain items are prohibited in international trade, and in other cases, Etsy sellers prefer not to ship their items outside certain regions.

Indicate your region preference by navigating to Your Account > Settings > Preferences. If you want to search among all available items, set your preference to Everywhere, which will reveal all items, even those that aren't available for shipment to your country.

Etsy sellers indicate where they're willing to ship by setting "shipping profiles." When they list items for sale, they indicate where they'll ship to, and the fees for various countries.

Language preference. The regional setting also sets your default language and currency preferences for Etsy. The site is available in English, French, Dutch, and German. You can adjust the setting by navigating to Your Account > Settings > Preferences.

Go on a shopping spree

If you want to be a great Etsy seller, one of the best ways to get ready is by going on a few Etsy shopping trips. Luckily, there are many inexpensive listings, so your education won't cost a fortune. However, your shopping activities will provide invaluable insights into how to compete as a seller. At the same time, you'll begin establishing your Etsy track record, which will be important when you begin selling your own items.

Put yourself in the buyer's shoes, so you can understand exactly what Etsy shoppers face when deciding to purchase, and what makes an item listing stand out. After making five or 10 purchases at Etsy, you'll have a clearer vision of which selling approaches will work best for you.

Let's buy something. Search and browse Etsy.com for something that strikes your fancy.

You can use Etsy's search bar to find items using keywords, such as "wool scarf." By default, the site's top search bar searches "Handmade" items, but you can reset the drop-down menu to limit the results to Vintage, Supplies, People, or Shops. Alternatively, you may choose all of them by selecting All Items.

On Etsy's homepage, Etsy.com, you can also browse by the list of categories in the left sidebar, or view "handpicked" items selected by Etsy's staff. And there's a row of items "recently listed" for sale.

The more search terms you use, the more relevant your results will be. For example, searching for "hat" will return thousands of listings for men's and women's hats, new and vintage, made from various materials, and in various sizes and styles. If you were shopping for something in particular, you might search for "Hat Fleece Leopard Print Stovepipe" to zero in on just what you're looking for.

If you want to eliminate certain items from your results, use the minus symbol (-) before a word. For example, searching for:

"hat, -purple"

will return items tagged "hat" but exclude those also tagged "purple." ("Tags," by the way, are descriptive words or phrases sellers add to their listings.)

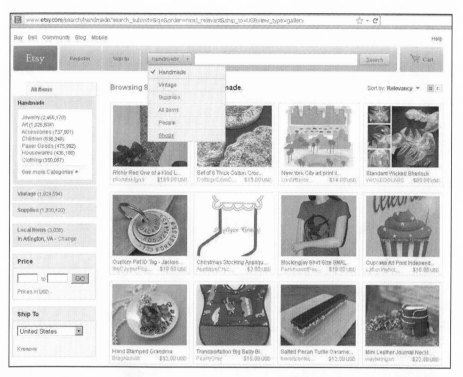

Selecting 'Supplies' from the drop-down menu will confine your search results to that top-level category. 'Handmade,' which is the default selection, will search all categories for handmade items. You can search all Etsy listings by selecting "All Items" from the menu. Another option is filtering by 'People,' which enables you to search for listings matching the given user name.

To search for a specific phrase, or tags consisting of multiple words, enclose the words in quotation marks. For example, searching for:

"solid gold"

will find items with that phrase in the listing title, or tagged with that exact phrase.

You can sort your search results by relevancy, price, and listing time by using the dropdown menu at the top of the search results.

Use multiple search operators and other refinements by using the "Advanced Search" form at Etsy.com/search_advanced.php.

www.etsy.com/search_advanced.php

Buy Sell Community Blog Mobile

Etsy   Register   Sign In   Handmade ▾

Home > Advanced Search

Advanced Item Search

Search for:

Search within:

Handmade Items	All Handmade Items
Vintage Items	Accessories
Art and Crafting Supplie	Art
All Items	Bags and Purses
	Bath and Beauty
	Books and Zines
	Candles
	Ceramics and Pottery

Include in search: (all)
☑ Item Tags   ☐ Item Materials
☑ Item Titles

Filter results by price:
$ [   ] to $ [   ]

Only show items from sellers who ship to:
[Choose country... ▾]

Sort by:
[Relevancy ▾]

View results as:
◉ Gallery
○ List

Search

Search Tips

• Use Categories for browsing

• Add descriptive words to narrow results.
women's red dress

• "Quotes" searches for phrases

• - (minus sign) eliminates items:
original painting -print -digital

• Sort by date listed or price

Etsy's 'advanced' search form offers more choices for filtering results.

Ways to Shop

Gift Ideas
Find gifts for friends

Colors
Shop by color

Treasury
Curated lists

Shop Local
Buy nearby

(At left) Four more ways to browse for items to buy on Etsy. These links appear at the bottom of the left sidebar on Etsy's home page.

"Gift Ideas" shows listings drawn from Facebook connections. "Colors" finds items based on their color. Treasuries are hand-curated lists of favorites. "Shop Local" lets you filter results by specific counties, towns, regions, or Zip codes.

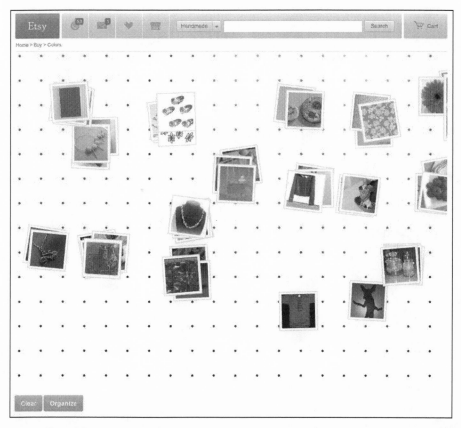

Etsy's Colors feature is a fancy way of presenting a palate of colors and shades, and finds matching handmade items, vintage goods, and supplies based on your selection. To visit the Colors tool directly, visit **Etsy.com/color.php**

Adding items to your cart

After you find an item you want to purchase, click the listing's green Add to Cart button. If you are not already signed in, Etsy will redirect you to the sign-in screen. If you continue shopping, you can always come back to your shopping card by clicking the cart icon on the top right of any page at Etsy.

If you're not certain whether you want to purchase the item immediately, you can bookmark it clicking on the red heart in the right sidebar of the item description page to add it to Your Favorites. In the same way, you can click on the red outlined heart to add the whole shop to Your Favorites.

Items in your shopping cart are grouped by shop. Each transaction is with a different seller.

Add Order Details. If you've got more than one item in your cart, items are grouped by shop. To purchase them all, you must place an order individually with each shop. You can add details to your order before paying. For example, in the "notes" section you can insert a message to the shopkeeper if you need to select a color, size, or other variation. Next you'll indicate the country where you want the items shipped, and you'll see an updated shipping and order total.

Payment method. For each shop, indicate how you'll pay, according to the options offered by the seller. Even if you're using the same payment method, such as PayPal, for more than one seller, each must be paid individually.

If you have a "shop coupon code," you can enter it here.

If you decide to abort the transaction, you can delete items from your cart by clicking the Remove link. Or instead of deleting it, you can click on the link Move to Favorites to move the item to Your Favorites for future reference.

A link for Contact Shop allows you to ask questions of the seller before you finalize the purchase. The link opens an Etsy Conversation, or "Convo," to the shopkeeper.

Once you've adjusted the order details to your liking, click the green Check Out button.

Payment and shipping via PayPal

PayPal is the most commonly used payment method on Etsy because it's relatively safe and convenient. PayPal allows quick settlement of transactions without having to share your bank account details with multiple parties. You just enter your PayPal password and authorize the payment.

One alternative to PayPal which Etsy began offering in 2012 is "Direct Checkout," which allows U.S. sellers to accept payments from customers using Visa, Mastercard/Eurocard, Discover Network, and American Express. For more information, see Etsy.com/checkout.

PayPal is free for buyers, and earns its revenue by seller fees. Buyers fund their purchases by linking their PayPal account to a credit card, debit card, or a checking or savings account.

If you're purchasing with PayPal, but don't have an account, you may open a PayPal account during the Etsy checkout process.

On the PayPal page, ensure your shipping address is correct. Click Continue, and you'll be returned to Etsy to complete your purchase.

Credit cards. Most Etsy shops accept PayPal. Even if you don't have a PayPal account, you can usually pay for items using a credit or debit card with PayPal's guest checkout service.

Checks, money orders and other payment methods. You'll be asked to enter a shipping address, at which point you can enter a new address on Etsy or select from a list of addresses you've used for previous purchases. Click Continue.

Bank transfers. If you select this option, you'll receive the shopkeeper's bank details, which will appear in Your Account > Purchases and in Etsy's email confirming the transaction. For this type of transaction, you'd need to ask your bank for instructions on how to send the money from your account to the seller's account. The seller won't receive your bank account details, but should receive the funds within two or three business days. Although the funds are withdrawn from your account immediately, some sellers don't ship items until they've received their bank's confirmation of the payment a few days later.

If your bank transfer is going to a foreign country, your bank—and perhaps the seller's bank—might charge a service fee. So if you're unsure, check with your bank beforehand, and ask the seller which currencies they accept.

Submit your order. Review your order details. If the seller is required to collect sales tax, you'll see this itemized in your summary. Here is another opportunity to ensure the shipping address on your order is correct.

If everything looks satisfactory, click the Submit Order button. You should see a confirmation message indicating the order is complete. An email with the order details will be sent to you and the shopkeeper, and the invoice is archived at Your Account > Purchases. If necessary, you can click a link on the invoice to communicate with the seller thorough an Etsy Convo or email.

Etsy Conversations (Convos)

Anytime you have a question for a seller, Etsy's built-in messaging system, Conversations, is a good way to communicate. It functions like email, and you can sort your messages into folders. Access this feature by clicking the envelope icon at the top of Etsy pages, or visit Etsy.com/conversations. When you receive a message, a number will appear over the envelope icon. If you wish, Etsy will send you an email notification each time you receive a Convo. Adjust the notification setting by visiting Your Account > Settings > Emails.

Leaving feedback

Your seller should send a message confirming your order and shipping details. After you receive the item, you can leave a "feedback" review of the seller's service and merchandise. Feedback serves as a record, or rating, of a member's experience of a transaction. If you've bought and sold on eBay or Amazon's Marketplace, Etsy's feedback system will look somewhat familiar.

Etsy's feedback system is key to an Etsy seller's reputation. You can rate the transaction as positive, neutral, or negative. A high feedback average helps sellers demonstrate their trustworthiness and consistency in pleasing buyers. Bad feedback serves to warn buyers away from unreliable, uncooperative sellers.

Etsy sellers can leave feedback for buyers, too—based on the overall experience and promptness of payment.

As a buyer, you can rate the service and merchandise received from an Etsy shop, and effectively recommend the shop to others—or not. You have 120 days to leave feedback following a transaction date.

As a shop owner	✚ Positive: 3900	⊘ Neutral: 63	▬ Negative: 31
Comment		Date	
▬ The ring is completely different, and I buy in another site with this person and never receive the merchandise		Jul 14, 2009	
▬ I ordered these item in May the 5th and still haven't recieved it, nor have I gotten a refund. After the first convo, the seller said she would resend them, but she didn't. Last convos have gone unanswered. This seller has over 25 negative feddbacks but it seems not to be a problem for someone who has also over 4.400 item sold. NEVER AGAIN!		Jul 6, 2009	
✚ super fast shipping. great ring!		Jul 2, 2009	
⊘ Took over a month to get. Very pretty though		Jul 2, 2009	
✚ Took a bit long to get here but they are lovely!		Jul 1, 2009	

Since purchases on Etsy are private, other members won't be able to see the individual feedback rating and message you leave for a seller, only an overall feedback average. For example, if an Etsy seller compiles 100 ratings including 95 positives and five negatives, their public feedback score is **Feedback: 100, 95% positive.** Neutral feedback doesn't affect the score.

Etsy members may keep their purchase history private, along with the feedback they've received from sellers. Shop owners, however, don't have this option—their sold-order history and feedback from shoppers is public.

Even with a feedback average of 99 percent positive, careful shoppers will be leery of buying from a seller whose recent history is pockmarked with negative ratings.

Here's how to leave feedback for a seller:

1. Visit Your Account > Feedback

2. **Click the** Items Awaiting Feedback tab.

3. **Rate the transaction and leave comments**. Click the button for "positive," "negative" or "neutral." Leaving an additional written comment is optional. (If you're contemplating leaving a negative or neutral feedback rating or comment because of a poor buying experience, give the seller a chance to respond before leaving the feedback. Since feedback affects their reputation, most sellers are happy to fix whatever problems have occurred,

as long as they're notified of the problem and have the opportunity.)

4. **Add a photo.** Adding an "appreciation photo" is optional.

5. **Submit your feedback.** Consider your feedback carefully because it's final—you won't be able to edit it or delete it later (except in a few circumstances explained below). When you're finished, click Submit.

Etsy regrets? Kiss and make up

Everyone makes mistakes. The "Kiss and Make Up" feature allows Etsians to change negative or neutral feedback if they're ultimately satisfied with the transaction.

Visit Your Account > Feedback > Completed Feedback, and you'll see a link for Kiss and Make Up under negative or neutral ratings you've submitted. If you click the link, an Etsy Convo is sent to extend the offer to your transaction partner (and you'll receive a copy). To complete the offer, both parties must agree to change their rating to positive.

Either transaction partner, buyer or seller, can initiate a Kiss and Make Up offer for transactions in which they've left negative or neutral feedback.

Deletion of inappropriate feedback

Etsy's staff rarely gets involved in disputes regarding feedback, no matter how justified one side's grievance might be. However, Etsy will delete abusive, harassing, or profane feedback when it's brought to their attention. This can occur, for example, if a feedback message contains certain private information, such as a member's telephone number.

Feedback that contains the following elements will be deleted by Etsy's staff:

• A member's email address, physical address, details about an Etsy investigation, or content of a private Etsy Convo.

• Mature, profane or racist language or images.

• Spam, links, scripts or advertising.

• Evidence of shilling (manipulation of feedback by using another Etsy account).

• The transaction is initiated solely for the purpose of leaving feedback.

- A negative or neutral rating was left in error for a different transaction.

- A negative or neutral rating refers to an unrelated transaction.

- Feedback submitted using the Kiss and Make Up feature includes negative comments or images.

- Negative or neutral feedback involves a complaint with Etsy or PayPal.

- A negative or neutral rating is left by a buyer who misunderstands the feedback system and leaves an unintended negative or neutral rating.

- Etsy receives a court order requesting removal of feedback.

Coupon and discount codes

Each Etsy shop can offer discounts by creating custom coupon codes. Shoppers can redeem the codes only by purchasing from the shop that created the code. If you buy multiple items from that seller, the code applies to the whole order.

Two codes are used at Etsy:

Percent Discount. Subtracts a flat percentage from your entire order with the participating shop, but does not apply to shipping.

Free shipping. Just like it sounds, this code removes shipping fees on an order at the participating shop. The seller might not offer free shipping on orders shipped to foreign countries.

To redeem a coupon code, enter it into the space provided at checkout, and click Apply. Your order price will be adjusted.

Shipping to a foreign country

In certain cases, PayPal's website won't allow you to provide a shipping address in a country other than where your account is registered. However, you can still enter a foreign shipping address on Etsy before finalizing your order. After clicking the Continue button at PayPal you'll return to Etsy to review your order. Click the link Change shipping address, and then enter the international address.

The new shipping address might affect the shipping and tax amounts, so you'll need to confirm the order again, then submit the order. The seller will receive an email explaining that you entered an international shipping address on Etsy.

Shipping to multiple locations. At checkout, you can only specify one shipping address for your Etsy order. To send some items to a different location, you must purchase them separately. As before, you'll enter the address during checkout. Notify the seller if the purchase is a gift being shipped directly to a friend.

Reporting nondelivery of an order

On rare occasions your item doesn't arrive within a reasonable amount of time and you're unable to reach the seller. In that case, file a report of nondelivery with Etsy, using this procedure:

1. Visit Your Account > Purchases. Locate the transaction involved, and click Invoice > Report a nondelivery.

2. Select the item(s) that haven't been delivered, then click Submit Report.

3. If you paid using PayPal, you'll need to file a claim for a refund with PayPal within 45 days of the payment.

Report a problem with an item you received

If you receive an incorrect or unsuitable item, try using email or an Etsy Convo to resolve the issue with the seller. You can also use Etsy's feedback system to review products and service. However, if there's a problem, you should contact the seller first and give them an opportunity to make things right.

If you paid with PayPal and received an unsatisfactory item—and the seller doesn't resolve the issue satisfactorily—you can file a claim with PayPal for "item not as described."

Flagging inappropriate listings

If you see an item for sale that violates Etsy policy, click the Report this item to Etsy link at the bottom of the page. Select one of the "reasons" from the menu:

- The item may not be handmade by the seller.

- The item may not be vintage (20+ years old).

- The item is not a supply for crafting or shipping.

- The item may be prohibited on Etsy.

- The listing is not labeled as mature content. (Items with "mature" images or themes must be tagged mature so that customers can filter out such material if they wish).

- The listing has an inaccurate category or tags.

- The listing links off-Etsy to buy the same items. (Sellers are prohibited from soliciting sales outside Etsy).

Add a brief explanation in the blank portion of the form (this is optional), and click Submit Report. A member of Etsy's staff will review the report and contact the seller or take other action if deemed necessary.

This "flagging" procedure is confidential—the seller won't know who has reported the item.

An entire shop can be flagged using the Report this shop to Etsy link on the shop's home page.

Revising your account information

If your contact information changes, you can easily update it on Etsy's Web site. For example, to change your email address, navigate to Your Account > Settings, and click the link regarding email.

To change your password, go to Your Account > Settings > Change password and follow the instructions.

If you forget your password, you can reset it from the Sign-In page. Enter the email address you used to register your account, and you'll receive an email from Etsy with a confirmation link. Clicking the link will send you to a page on Etsy where you can enter your new password. You'll receive another email confirming the change.

The password reset email will be sent from this address: lostpassword@mail.etsy.com. If you don't receive the message promptly, check your spam folder or add the address to your list of approved addresses.

Passwords are case-sensitive at Etsy, so ensure your computer's Caps Lock button isn't depressed when you sign in.

Sellers can change their billing preference by visiting Your Account > Settings > Billing, where your credit card, phone number, and billing address is stored. If you need to change the address or phone number, you'll need to validate your credit card again, which is a security precaution taken by Etsy.

SELLER PROFILE: Wooly Baby

Josie Marsh of Kennett Square, Pa., fashions baby and kids' slippers from recycled wool sweaters, a neat twist on the eco-friendly upcycling craze.

See Etsy.com/shop/woolybaby.

How did you get started?

When my daughter was learning to walk, I wanted some high-topped, wool, leather-bottomed slippers. I couldn't find any. Being an engineer with nothing to do during my baby's naptimes, I set out to make my own.

I was raised by resourceful, creative hippies who made everything we needed.

My mom had given me some felted wool sweater diaper covers. That gave me the idea of using felted wool sweaters to make slippers and wool pants. I listed a few of these on Etsy, and had my first sale within a few weeks. After that, nothing could stop me!

Are you a one-person shop, or do you have a partner?

I have one near-full-time seamstress who is a subcontractor for me. She takes the work to her home.

How has your Etsy business affected your family and career?

I was an engineer before my daughter was born, but have not been inspired to go back to that work—yet.

During the first two years of Wooly Baby, it was tough to balance my business with raising my daughter, getting exercise, etc. But with the help of my seamstress, I have been much better at that this year.

How has your business evolved and weathered the tough economy?

I began my business in November 2008, so I haven't really experienced NOT being in a tough economic environment! My sales have grown at about 40 percent year over year, and I'm extremely happy with that. I'm continually trying to figure out how to grow my business.

How do you attract customers and get repeat business?

My biggest advantage is there are very few people selling wool slippers on Etsy, so I am fairly easy to find. I strive to take good photographs and treat my customers well. If I make a mistake, I learn from it and try to prevent it from happening again.

The quality of my slippers has improved enormously since I began. Most of my design changes have been initiated from customer feedback.

What percentage of your business is online?

Online is 76 percent, craft shows are 17 percent (I only do a few per year), retail is 4 percent, and "other" is 3 percent.

Wool Baby Slippers, Eco friendly & Handmade, Sizes 6-18, 12-24 months, Lamb to School

zoom

When my daughter was learning to walk on our slippery wood floors, I created high-ankled, soft-soled, non-skid slippers like these for her. She wore them constantly and now I offer these soft slippers to keep your little one warm and sure-footed all winter long. They are handmade from a charcoal gray, recycled, felted, 100% lambswool or 100% merino wool

How do you determine pricing?

I carefully calculate how much time and materials go into making my slippers. Sorting through thrift stores to find sweaters, and going to Laundromats to felt my materials are a big part. I pay myself and my subcontractor a modest hourly wage.

What's your take on paid advertising?

I have not tried any paid advertising. I pretty much have all the business I can handle.

How can a newcomer to Etsy be successful?

Be unique. There are so many sellers on Etsy, if you don't stand out in some way, you're not going to have a good experience selling. It's just too hard to be found. You either need to sell something that very few people are selling, or you need to make your line of jewelry or your T-shirt unique. Fill a niche. Don't be afraid to be weird. If you like it, there are others who will, too. Don't try to please everyone.

OPEN FOR BUSINESS!

OK, we've experienced Etsy from the buyer's side. Now, are you ready for some selling? You can sell on Etsy using the same account you registered as a buyer. The user name you selected when registering at Etsy also becomes your shop name, but you can change it. Your shop has its own Web address based on your user name: http://username.etsy.com

This way works, too: http://www.etsy.com/shop/username.

To start selling, you'll need to "upgrade" your account by clicking on the "Sell" link in the top gray bar of the site and follow the instructions. Upgrading to seller status requires a valid credit or debit card.

Identify yourself on Etsy

 You have a couple of options for identifying yourself on Etsy. You can be represented by a user name, which can also serve as your Shop name. If you wish, you can also display your real name, so it appears with your user name whenever you participate in Etsy community teams or forums, or post other content on the site. After you become a seller, your participation throughout Etsy will serve a dual purpose—identifying you personally, plus helping promote your shop as you participate in the community.

Adding your real name aids navigation for people who meet you on Etsy. If they want to see your shop, they can click your shop name. If they want to discover more about you personally, they can click on your name to visit your profile.

By default, Etsians who don't own a shop are represented by their full name, unless they decide, for privacy or other reasons, to remove it from their profile. If you'd rather display only a user name and shop name on Etsy, you can remove your real name from your Etsy profile by visiting Etsy.com/your/profile.

What's in a name?

If you're still deciding on a shop name, choose a name that passes the "radio test." That means it's easy to say, easy to spell, and easy to remember. Keep it short and sweet. JanesArt is a lot better than drawingsandpaintingsbyjane, don't you think? Keep it to the essentials, and use capital letters to sharpen the meaning (although the address isn't case-sensitive when you type it in your browser's address bar.)

What sellers on Etsy do you admire? Why do you remember them? Figure out how they were ingrained in your mind, and how you'll put your own twist on things.

Be careful not to use a trademarked name or expression. For this, you'll need to do some research—ignorance is no excuse for breaking the law or violating Etsy's rules. A Google search will alert you to potential problems, but if you're in doubt, consult an attorney.

Remember that your first choice for a shop name may already be taken on Etsy, so be prepared to brainstorm some variations or alternatives.

If you rename your shop, it's automatically assigned a new URL based on the revised name. Fortunately, the URL based on your previous name automatically forwards visitors to your new shop's URL.

If you have two separate product lines, should you maintain a different Etsy account for each? Perhaps, if the styles and personalities are entirely different. Just be sure to disclose both shops in your profile and shop announcements, which is required by Etsy. You will need to use a separate email address for each Etsy account.

Some Etsians maintain separate accounts for buying and selling. Multiple accounts provide more leeway to criticize sellers who provide substandard items or service. True enough, some sellers who receive complaints take it personally, and retaliate by posting negative information about buyers. Even worse, an irate seller might purchase an item from the complaining buyer's shop, just to provide an opportunity for retaliatory insults and negative feedback.

So a separate buying account can insulate a seller from becoming entangled in such grudges. But Etsy doesn't encourage this because it creates the potential for confusion and, for the unscrupulous, an opportunity for troublemaking and "shilling"—buying from yourself to inflate your track record. So, separate accounts aren't prohibited, but they require special disclosures. If you have multiple Etsy accounts, you must list all your user names in your bio for each account, it's mandatory. And separate accounts require unique user names and email addresses.

Privacy and using your real name

Some people, whether they're buying or selling, are hesitant to use their real name on Etsy. For some, it's nothing personal against Etsy. They just resist putting any personal information on the Internet when it's not absolutely necessary. Although displaying your real name is optional, many top-flight sellers actually prefer to have their name out there. They believe displaying their name enhances credibility by demonstrating you're a real person and stand behind what you sell. It all comes down to personal preference. Many longtime, successful Etsy sellers display only a nickname as their user name and shop name.

If you change your mind about this later, you can edit or delete your name from public view by navigating to Your Account > Profile and changing the form.

Changing your Etsy avatar. If you haven't yet uploaded a professional-looking, memorable avatar that suits your business, this is a good time to do so. A good avatar will help reinforce your store "brand" wherever people encounter you on Etsy—at your Shop, your profile, and when you participate on Etsy teams and discussion boards.

The right avatar depends on your business and personality. Some people use a portrait of themselves, an image of a favorite item or signature product, or a logo. Sellers sometimes use a version of their Shop logo, or a temporary icon to signify they're having a promotion.

To upload your avatar, go to Your Account > Profile. Click the Browse button and select the image file from your computer. Etsy will convert the image to a square image, 75 pixels by 75 pixels. If the picture you upload isn't square, it might appear distorted, or be cropped at the sides.

If you're not already familiar with an image-editing tool such as Photoshop, the upcoming section about Etsy banners will provide information about easy-to-use online tools and services for creating avatars and banners.

Shop announcement

This text is previewed just below your shop banner. Here you can announce sales or promotions. Or you can simply welcome shoppers and briefly describe your craft or specialty. Shoppers may click a link to read the full text. There's no limit on how much text you can insert here, but don't overdo it. Your visitor might be in a buying mood, so don't bog them down now with minutia. Save the details for your profile, shop policies, and listing descriptions.

To add or edit your Shop Announcement, visit Your Account > Info & Appearance. Click Save Changes.

Message to Buyers. This feature enables you to automatically insert a brief message in the transaction notice sent to buyers when they make a purchase from your shop. You might include a thank you, a reminder about your shipping method, and other shop policies. Add or change your Message to Buyers by visiting Your Account > Info & Appearance. Click Save.

Beef up your profile

Part of the draw of Etsy is it allows buyers to feel a personal connection with the designer and seller of a craft. That's why you should give special attention to filling out your profile with details like these:

- Your avatar, or profile photo

- Your name

- Gender (optional)

- City

- Birthday (optional)

- Favorite materials

- Favorite items

There's also a box labeled About where you can insert a short biography. Here, you can be brief or long-winded. Adding a biography is optional, but remember that if you're a seller, such information boosts your credibility and can pique the interest of shoppers. Add details about your qualifications, experience, awards, and other pertinent details. If you've been selling at regional craft fairs for 10 years, say so. Have you been written up in your local newspaper? Mention it, and provide a link to the article, if possible. Mention your hobbies, your passions, where you attended school. If you publish a blog or website, provide the link.

If you have lots of details in your biography, present them in bits, which makes the bio easier to read. Begin a new paragraph every few lines, instead of having one huge block of text.

And for goodness sakes, proofread your biography, and get a few other people to proofread it, too. Nothing is worse than a biography marred with misspellings and grammatical errors. You want your profile to have an air of easy professionalism. But if your biography suggests "I'm sloppy and care-less," it won't win over many buyers.

Get started with your profile by visiting Your Account, then click Public Profile in the left sidebar. Enter your details, and click Save changes.

Add a banner to your shop

Once you've upgraded your account to seller status, you're entitled to add a banner to be displayed atop your shop. It should mesh with your shop in terms of color, branding, and style. You can also have multiple banners in a rotation based on season or special promotions.

Having an eye-catching, professional-looking banner is a must—and something you should revisit later, if you develop a better design for your banner, or your style of merchandise changes.

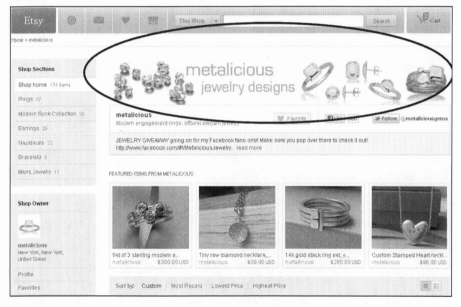

Home page for the Etsy shop **Metalicious**. In this illustration, the shop banner is cir-cled to show its position. Underneath the banner are two text areas—the shop title, then the shop announcement. Next is the Shop's featured items.

Many Etsy sellers base their avatar on their shop banner. Regardless of whether the avatar and banner originate from the same artwork or design, they should certainly mesh, and not clash.

Etsy requires your banner to be a certain type of an image file, formatted as a .jpg, .gif or .png, sized at 760 by 100 pixels, and a resolution of 72 dpi, or dots per inch. If your image file deviates from these specifications, your shop banner may appear fuzzy or distorted.

Upload your banner image by visiting Your Account > Info & Appearance. Click Browse, find the file on your computer, and click Save at the bottom.

You can create a shop banner by using image-editing software such as Photoshop or Gimp, but you don't have to be a computer geek or a design whiz to create a nice banner.

Tweak your shop title

You're allowed up to 66 characters, letters and numbers only, to describe your shop in its title. Edit the shop title by visiting Your Account > Info & Appearance. Change the text, then click Save.

Think of your shop title as a slogan or tagline that helps describe your business. For example, a maker of cheeky, fancy purses on Etsy might use the shop title, "Classy bags for classy broads." That's OK—it has personality—but not many keywords. A great shop title is memorable, while squeezing in as many accurate, descriptive keywords as possible. Here's a better shop title: "Handmade leather and fabric bags and clutches for your every day."

If your business focus changes as you introduce more lines of materials or merchandise, revisit your decision on your shop's title. It's the first and most basic element to enhance your Search Engine Optimization (SEO), which helps new customers find your shop using Google and other search tools. We'll cover this in more detail in the upcoming section, "Put Google to work for you."

State your shop policies

Shop policies aren't mandatory, but they're expected by experienced Etsy shoppers. Having a well-designed set of shop policies helps set buyer expectations, and can prevent repetitive questions from prospective customers. So, under what circumstances do you accept returns? Is there a time limit? Do you charge people a "restocking fee" on exchanges? Who pays return shipping costs? Do you require payment within 24 hours of a purchase? What about sales tax? Explain these details on your Shop Policy page, and it will be there in case of a dispute. But don't regurgitate them all in your Shop Announcement or profile—those are the places to talk about you and what you're selling, what's on sale, and what's new. There's a link to your Policies within each listing in your Etsy shop.

At a minimum, your shop policies should explain your terms of sale—what forms of payment you accept, your shipping procedure, and your policy on handling returns. Your policies page is a great opportunity to explain how you conduct business. You want to give people a firm idea of what to expect. The right details can enhance your credibility and help close a lot of sales. On the other hand, you don't want to sound defensive or overly strict,. You don't want to give people a lot of reasons NOT to buy from you.

For example, lots of beginning sellers decide, foolishly, to be super-strict about returns. With a straight face, they might say, "Returns must be received within five days of purchase." Technically, this is OK, but it's a turnoff for shoppers. Although Etsy allows each seller to set policy on returns and exchanges, unnecessarily tough policies don't really discourage returns, they discourage sales. Put yourself in the customer's shoes. They're being asked to buy something, sight unseen, from someone they probably don't know. A reasonable return policy reassures customers that you stand behind what you sell. On the other hand, sellers usually don't offer exchanges or refunds on custom-made items, and buyers don't generally expect it. Otherwise, consider returns as part of the cost of doing business. If you're doing an all-around good job, your rate of returns should be way below 5 percent of your business. You can't please everyone.

And, of course, your shop's policies don't override Etsy's company policies, and they can't contradict national or local consumer laws.

Add or edit your Shop Policies by visiting Your Account > Info & Appearance > Policies. Click Save. There's a template for these headings: Welcome Message, Payment, Shipping, Refunds, Additional Information, and Seller Information, which may be required if you are selling in the European Union. If you leave a section blank, the heading won't appear on your Policies page.

A reminder about returns: Etsy won't refund selling fees you racked up on a sale, regardless of whether you accept the item's return and refund the buyer. Apparently, Etsy is worried that unscrupulous sellers would "refund" too many purchases as a way of avoiding Etsy's fees. It's unfair to reputable sellers, but Etsy writes the rules on its site.

Other policy details to consider

Will you ship a gift if the ship-to address conflicts with the PayPal address? It's a common request—lots of gifts are bought on Etsy—but it also could be a sign of fraud. Beware especially when shipping expensive items, particularly if the buyer has no track record on Etsy as a reliable buyer or seller. PayPal's seller protection policy can be voided if you ship to a different address.

More details to consider:

- What kind of shipping service do you use? The U.S. Postal Service? Priority Mail or regular parcel rate? UPS? Do you provide a tracking number? Do you upgrade shipping in certain cases? Can the customer pay extra for next-day delivery?

● Do you insure your parcels? Do you charge extra for insurance? How much?

● How do you package your items? Do you use recycled packing materials? Let your buyers know what they can expect.

● Do you offer a local pickup option for nearby buyers? (Many sellers believe this is more trouble than it's worth.)

● Do you ship internationally?

● When do you ship? Within 24 hours of receiving payment? Within three days?

On the subject of returns, it pays to exhibit grace, on both the buying and selling sides. If you're returning something to an Etsy seller, remember that it's not the same as a return to a mass retailer or department store. A return from an Etsy customer is sometimes taken personally. The crafter usually did their best on the item you've sent back. If they're a beginner who has poured their heart and soul into their item, and mustered the courage to sell it, a return can be tough. The seller won't feel any better about it if you insult their taste or abilities. Likewise, sellers must take their occasional lumps because they can't please everyone.

The key is to accept things (according to the rules), and move on. Don't fret about all the things you can't control.

Example of a good shop policy

Here's an example of a good shop policy by Josie Marsh, proprietor of Wooly Baby. It's clear and to the point. It helps shoppers find what they want and avoid ordering what they don't want. If they need more information, she tells them where to get it. You can tell that Josie is a busy seller, has contemplated just about every conceivable ordering snafu, and proactively avoids them with a clear, detailed shop policy:

WoolyBaby Shop Policies:

Welcome

AVAILABLE SIZES: [here she provides detailed instructions on measuring kids' feet].

TIPS: Wooly Baby slippers are meant to be roomy and tend to fit wide feet well. If in between sizes, order up.

FIND YOUR SIZE: To find the slippers that I have in stock in your size, enter your size (such as "12-24 months", "kids 9.5" or "women 8') into the search bar at the top of my shop. Be sure to use the sizes that I have listed above!

QUANTITY: If I show more than one in stock and you would like to purchase more than one pair, please Convo me to adjust the quantity before you place your order.

CUSTOM SIZES: There is about 1/2" between each of my standard sizes, so I hope that these sizes can fit most feet!

Did I mention ... please measure your feet if possible! More info here... http://www.wooly-baby.com/sizechart.html

Payment

PAYPAL: PayPal is my preferred method of payment and must be received before I begin working on your order. Please pay within 2 days or your order may be canceled.

NO PAYPAL ACCOUNT?

You can still pay if you don't have a PayPal account. Copy and paste this link for more information: http://www.etsy.com/help/article/361

Or you may call me and I can process your credit card over the phone.

NEW TO ETSY?

Use this tutorial to help you through the checkout process:

http://www.etsy.com/help/article/339

Shipping

WITHIN THE US: All items are shipped First Class and include tracking and delivery confirmation (2-5 days shipping time).

INTERNATIONAL: Items are shipped First Class Parcel but tracking is not available. Shipping time is typically 5-10 days, but can be up to 3 weeks or more. International buyers are responsible for customs fees.

LOSS/DAMAGE: Wooly Baby is not responsible for any items lost or damaged in shipment.

WHEN? I ship orders on Tuesdays and Fridays (early in the morning). In-stock slippers will ship on the next Tuesday or Friday after your order; custom orders ship within the lead time posted in my shop announcement. Please contact me if you need your order shipped more quickly.

ADDRESS: I use PayPal to create shipping labels (within the US), so please notify me if you do not want your order to be shipped to the address on your PayPal account. I can ship to a gift recipient if requested (and send a gift note).

PACKAGING: My items are packed in recycled (30% post consumer) brown paper in a plastic recyclable envelope. My tags are also made from recycled paper.

Please contact me if you have any special shipping request!

Refunds and Exchanges

I welcome your feedback and am serious about using it to improve my slippers. If Wooly Baby makes a mistake, I will replace your slippers and pay First Class shipping costs. If the slippers are the wrong size or you do not like the slippers, you may return them within 30 days for an exchange (you pay all shipping costs). The item must not be visibly worn. Please contact me before returning anything from Wooly Baby or if you have any questions.

Additional Policies and FAQs

GIFT CARDS: If you are mailing directly to a gift recipient, I am happy to include a free gift card. Just mention it in the "Notes to WoolyBaby" when you check out (along with your gift message).

CUSTOM ORDERS: Sorry, I cannot make custom orders at this time [during the second half of the year]. I can accept custom orders February through July. Typically this means making slippers in a color/size that you do not see in my shop. See the SIZING information above about ordering a non-standard size.

NEWSLETTER: Go to http://www.wooly-baby.com/email.html to sign up for my email newsletter. I send out updates and sale announcements about 4-5 times a year.

FACEBOOK: www.facebook.com/WoolyBaby

QUESTIONS: If you have other question, they may be answered on my website (http://www.wooly-baby.com/questions.html) or you may contact me with an Etsy "conversation".

All items in the Wooly Baby shop are designed by me, Josie Marsh. Thank you for supporting my eco-friendly business!

-- Josie

Pricing your items

OK, how much should you charge for your creations? As much as possible, right?

Average market price. Many beginning sellers price their items in line with similar items from other sellers. They make a quick survey of listings from sellers offering similar items to arrive at an average market price. That's OK, but don't be too hasty; many new Etsy sellers make the mistake of undervaluing their work. They set their prices too low, thinking it will spur sales. Instead, low prices can actually hurt the sales of fine crafts.

If you consistently under-price, you'll create two problems. First, you'll lower the perceived value of your work. When customers see a price that seems very low, they might assume something is wrong with it. Instead of increasing your sales, lower prices can retard your sales. Secondly, rock-bottom prices attract lots of—how can I put this diplomatically?—problem customers. For example, let's imagine you're selling personalized screen-printed T-shirts. Because you're just starting on Etsy and you want to rapidly build a customer base and feedback record, you decide to initially sell your shirts at $3 apiece, just your cost of materials. And you might assume that every buyer will be thrilled to buy a personalized T-shirt for $3. But believe me, not everyone will be happy. In fact, you'll probably attract more unhappy customers than if you sold the same shirts for $15. The "bargain" buyers tend to gripe much more frequently than regular buyers. They'll complain about the material or the color, they'll claim the shirt has an odd odor, they'll complain that shipping was too expensive or took too long. Fortunately, difficult customers are in the distinct minority. But you'll attract a large share of them by offering rock-bottom prices. And, believe me, these "problem" customers are harder to deal with than regular buyers who might have a legitimate complaint.

Your goal over time should be to come up with new, unique designs, which will give you more freedom and confidence to consistently raise prices and, hence, your profits. Let some other poor seller have the "bargain" buyers.

Figure your costs like a pro

If you're serious about making your Etsy shop a real business, you must consider all your costs of material, overhead, and your time spent crafting each piece, as well as your time managing your shop and marketing. Include your own labor (many crafters figure on $10 to $30 per hour), plus materials (materials, office supplies, and packaging materials), and overhead like Etsy and PayPal fees, office space, and utilities.

OK, let's assume you know your costs. How much should you charge for each item? Many crafters have a simple formula for figuring their wholesale and retail rates: They multiply their costs times two, then do it again. It's a good rule of thumb. For example, let's say a piece costs you $15 to make, including materials, labor and overhead. Using the "times two" formula, you'd set a wholesale price of $30—that's what you'd charge retailers who want to carry your item. (You say you're a beginner, and don't have wholesale accounts? Figure it anyway—we're thinking big.)

Now, your **retail price**—what you're charging your Etsy buyer—is "times two" again. For our example, we'll multiply our "wholesale" price of $30 by 2, and arrive at $60 retail. That pricing formula gives you plenty of room to knock $10 off your price for the occasional sale.

Certainly you can't charge higher prices on Etsy for run-of-the-mill products. So if you're competing in a hotly competitive category—say, fabric iPhone cases under $10—your product must have some special quality. Whether it's higher-quality material, a unique design, a familiar name, or superior service, you must have *something* the competition doesn't have. Retailers call this your "unique selling proposition," or USP.

Tiered pricing. Tiered pricing is another good pricing strategy for Etsy sellers. Tiered pricing simply means you have items offered at different price points. For example, if most of your Etsy items are priced around $100, it's really smart to include some lower-priced items at $10 or $20. That allows a new customer to sample your shop without risking an arm and a leg. Likewise, if you're doing great selling low-end items priced at about $15, it's really smart to develop some items priced higher, say $75, $100 or more. If lots of people love your stuff, some of those are going to want to buy your higher-end items, too.

The Etsy Fee Calculator shows exactly how much Etsy, PayPal and postage fees will bite into your profits. In this example, we've assumed a selling price of $35, a shipping and handling fee of $5, postage costs of $3, and material costs of $8. Given this data, the site automatically calculates your total Etsy and PayPal fees, and your profit of $26.11. Don't forget to consider all labor and advertising costs and costs of your packing materials. The site, written by developer Ryan Olbe, is at **Rolbe.com/etsy**.

Loss leaders. If you wanted to be particularly aggressive with tiered pricing, you could add a "loss leader" item or line. You might sell something at cost, or even lower, as a way of attracting more customers. For example, if you sell assortments of handmade soap, you might offer low-priced miniature bars as a method for getting new customers to sample your products. Once your customers have a chance to experience your good service and products, they'll be apt to buy more.

Just don't make *most* of your items "loss leaders" or you'll never turn a profit.

Don't be cheap, you're worth it

Avoid bargain-bin pricing, and your profits will be healthier. Here are some additional ways of enhancing the perceived value of your items:

- **Use high-grade materials and advanced techniques.** Etsy shoppers will usually pay more for an item constructed of fine materials and top-notch handiwork. Making your items appear more exclusive will enable you to sell more items at higher prices.

- **Use elaborate packaging.** Spending an extra dollar on a fancy box or ribbons makes your items seem more special. Sending your items in a bubble mailer sends the wrong message: "This item isn't valuable enough to be sent in a protective box."

- **Create a series.** Target collectors by creating a numbered series of items, or a series based on a theme like kittens, jaguars or ducks. Developing a series adds value to your work.

- **Your reputation.** Your track record as a reliable, friendly seller will win you many sales. This is where customer feedback comes in, demonstrating that you ship the promised items promptly, and go the extra mile to fix any problems that might arise.

- **A guarantee.** An unconditional satisfaction guarantee helps you establish buyer confidence. If you don't have a long track record, a strong guarantee will compensate. Customers feel much freer to buy if they know they can return an item when necessary without a hassle.

Choose your accepted forms of payment

Now, indicate which payment methods you'll accept for your sales. Visit Your Account > Shipping & Payment > Payment Methods. You can select PayPal, personal checks, money orders, bank transfers, and "other." Once you decide which payment forms you accept, your choices will automatically apply to each of your shop's item listings.

Accepting PayPal is a no-brainer. It's not perfect, but it's the most popular payment method for a reason—it's relatively safe and convenient. You'll pay some transaction fees, but you'd lose lots of sales if you didn't accept PayPal, perhaps most of them. You'll need to enter your PayPal-registered email address into your Etsy account.

To accept checks or money orders, you'll need to enter your mailing address so customers can mail their payments. The use of checks and money orders declines every year, but some customers prefer them to PayPal; old habits die hard. If you accept checks and money orders, they present some risks in the form of counterfeiting and bounced payments. Some sellers delay shipment for a week or so after a receiving a check or money order, to ensure the payment clears their bank. Of course, if a buyer has a long track record as an Etsy buyer, chances are their payment will be good.

Bank transfers are a more common form of payment outside the United States. To accept them, you need to provide your account holder name, bank name and account number, and routing number. Some U.S. sellers are uncomfortable providing these details. To accept payments from another country, you'll need to provide more information, such as a Swift ID or IBAN number. Bank transfers have other disadvantages: They can generate bank fees, and some banks won't even process them for deposit to a regular bank account. Because of these drawbacks, some sellers, particularly in the United States, refuse to accept them, and require PayPal for overseas purchases. The advantage with PayPal is that when the seller and buyer are using different currencies, PayPal automatically converts the currencies for buyer and seller.

Spotting scams on Etsy

Etsy is a great place to buy and sell. But like any big community, Etsy attracts some crooks and deadbeats. By far, the most common scam involves counterfeit cashier's checks and money orders. A typical scam: A new customer offers to make a purchase worth a large sum, from a few hundred dollars to several thousand dollars. Often a premium is offered in exchange for rush shipping. Two or more of these three factors—a large order, rush shipping, and a money order or cashier's check—is a red flag. Ensure that such payments have cleared your bank—which can take more than a week, especially for overseas payments—before shipping your merchandise.

Because scams involving money orders and cashier's checks are so common, some Etsy sellers simply don't accept these types of payments. These shenanigans aren't unique to Etsy; they occur via telephone, email, and at other Web marketplaces. However, too many victims are new Etsy sellers, who are understandably eager to make their first big sale, and perhaps too trusting of unfamiliar buyers.

Sometimes legitimate buyers will offer to pay cash, and ask to pick up an item in person instead of having it shipped. This is risky for several reasons. At best, out-of-the-ordinary transactions are inconvenient and take valuable time away from your business. At worst, your personal safety is jeopardized by meeting strangers for a cash transaction. Many sellers flatly refuse such offers because they've learned from experience that such buyers often fail to appear at the agreed time, or ask for an additional discount because it's a cash transaction with no shipping costs.

Operate a collective shop

Some of the best businesses are built upon partnerships. Perhaps you're already working with someone—you handle the design, and your partner handles the construction. In the craft business, two or more people working together can form a "collective," and it's not uncommon on Etsy. However, there are strict rules on Etsy about governing collective shops. The individual who initially registers the account with their credit is held responsible for all the account activity—and the bills. More details about the special rules governing collectives are in the "Mind Your Manners" chapter of this book.

SELLER PROFILE: Indulge Your Shelf

Laurie Jackson of Peyton, Colo., sells both handmade items and vintage finds on Etsy. See **Etsy.com/shop/IndulgeYourShelf** and **Etsy.com/shop/LeavesAndLace**.

How did you get started?

I have two Etsy shops: one for vintage, and one for handmade textile and paper crafts made from vintage materials. I've been collecting vintage forever, and frequenting thrift and antique stores as a hobby. I began to notice fantastic items in thrift stores priced far below their value, so I bought them to resell online. I began with eBay, but when their fees became small-shop unfriendly, I switched to Etsy.

My handmade products were a natural offshoot of my thrift shopping. I collected beautiful linens, laces, buttons, and salvaged vintage jewelry and then put it together, repurposing it into something I loved. Friends began asking to buy some items, and the business grew from there.

Why do you operate two shops instead of one?

When I started, I listed both vintage and handmade items in the same shop, but I decided it was better to separate them. My handmade stuff got lost among the vintage listings.

Also, Etsy has two distinct communities—people who sell handmade items and supplies, and those who sell vintage. By having two shops with their own focus and identity, I can participate with both communities.

How do you fit in Etsy with family and work life?

When I began selling on Etsy, I worked outside of the home. I photographed and listed my items on weekend mornings, packaged my sales and printed postage in the evenings, and mailed them on the way to work. Later, I became a full-time student, and continued running my shops in the same way. Now, as a stay-at-home mom, I have more time, and dedicate a couple of days a week to my shops.

How has your business evolved since you started, and how have you managed the tough economy?

I've learned a lot about the vintage business and made some changes along the way. When I started out, I bought vintage items if they had a great price, regardless of my personal opinion about the item. I soon learned items sometimes don't sell, and I'd be stuck with them. So I gave myself the guideline of not buying something if I didn't love it myself, no matter how great a deal it was. This helped me develop a "style" for my shop, and a reputation as someone with an eye for great stuff.

I've also moved away from stocking breakable items and large artwork in my vintage shop. Although they sell well, they are expensive to package and ship, and take up too much storage room.

Vintage, Like New, Josef Originals March Birthday Girl with Original Tag

ᵖ zoom

A beautiful, like new figurine by Josef Originals -- this is the March birthday girl with blue birthstone flower centers. She is in amazing condition for her age. Stands ~4" x 4" diameter.

All of the items in this shop are vintage and sold as is, so look closely at the photos to be sure you love it before purchasing!

The tough economic climate has forced me to produce fewer and smaller items in my handmade shop. I've also begun making some items that can be used as supplies, rather than finished products because supplies can be priced lower.

How do you find items?

I do best when I limit my buying trips to once or twice per week. I often wait several weeks to unpack, clean, photograph and list vintage products. That way, I'm processing several large bags full of items all at once.

Likewise, with my handmade shop, I set aside time to make several pieces at once. All of my products are collage-like, made from many raw materials. So I like to make a big mess all at once, and get a lot of product out of it.

How do you attract customers and get repeat business?

Etsy encourages "community" on the website, and by marking items and shops as favorites, and establishing circles of users, my items appear on many activity pages. Because I take the time to tag my products creatively and photograph them in a pleasing way, they're included in many Treasuries, which are a great showcase. Participating in circles and creating Treasuries of my own are reciprocal activities to help promote my fellow Etsians.

I also participate in Etsy Teams, such as Etsy Beagles (Etsians who own Beagles), Etsians of Facebook, and the vintage groups Collectorsville, Hoarders Anonymous, and Vintage Lovers. Our teams often hold team sales, where we promote each other and share Etsy tips and information on the forums. Etsians of Facebook "like" each other, so their Etsy shop Facebook pages get plenty of exposure.

Can you share other promotional techniques?

I publicize both shops through my blog, IndulgeYourShelf.blogspot.com. On the sidebars I have Etsy widgets called "Minis" to showcase current items in my shop. On the blog I write about some of my best purchases, mentioning that they're available in my shop and including a link. I've developed a network of online friends, many of whom have their own blogs, and I drive traffic to my blog by commenting on their blogs, which link back to my own. When one of my products appears in a Treasury, I put a link to that Treasury on my Facebook page.

When I attend artistic events, I pass out business cards to people who share my interests. Keeping in touch with previous customers and people I've met at art events have been the most successful methods for increasing my sales.

Great customer service and friendly communication brings repeat business.

How do you benefit from blogging?

It enables people to get to know me a bit, and they feel better buying from someone they "know." It also establishes me as an expert of sorts as I share information about vintage items and link to other people and resources. It creates an atmosphere of joy and fun around whatever item I'm writing about.

What percentage of your business is online versus offline?

My business is 100 percent online. Because I live in the Midwest, most of my customers are in the Southeast or on the west coast—prices are lower here, so they're still getting value, even with my shipping costs. I prefer selling online instead of locally.

What is your procedure for valuing and pricing items?

I learned by trial and error what prices the Etsy market will bear. From this, I developed a formula for how much I can spend on my stock, which helps with my buying decisions. I've also learned how to buy at auction, which is the very best way to increase profits in the vintage business.

I value my items by paying attention to pricing in the antique stores I visit, and by researching them online. I often check eBay prices as well as Etsy's.

Have you tried paid advertising, like Google Adwords or the Etsy ads?

I've tried Google and Facebook ads and didn't see any tangible results, so I don't think they're worth it for a small business like mine. I tried placing an ad in the Etsy Showcase and, likewise, it was expensive and unsuccessful. These advertising tools might pay off for someone with a unique idea or product they need to publicize, buy not for the kind of products I sell.

CREATE AND EDIT YOUR LISTINGS

OK, now we're in the belly of the selling beast. We'll take a quick overview of the listing process. Later in the book, we'll revisit each step in detail.

When you're selling on Etsy, each of your items is presented on a page called a "listing," which contains several elements you can specify and edit:

- Item Details

- Product images (as many as five)

- Item Title

- Item Description

- Shop Section

- Attributes

- Tags

- Materials

- Price

- Quantity

- Shipping Information

List an item

OK, you've got your Etsy shop set up, you've upgraded to seller status, and you've uploaded your shop banner. Now, select the first item you're ready to sell.

1. Let's list an item for sale.

Click Your Shop > Add New Item

Now, broadly classify your item. Using the drop-down menu on Etsy's site, you'll identify who made the item, what it is, and when it was made.

2. Categorize your item.

Now you'll select an Etsy's top-level category from the drop-down menu.

3. Add images.

You can include as many as five images for each listing. To get started, click the add photos icon. You can browse your computer for the image files you want to upload.

Your images should be at least 570 pixels wide to have a sufficient level of sharpness and detail. You can take an adequate photo with most digital cameras and newer camera-equipped smartphones.

Taking great product photos is an art itself, and we'll explore it in detail later.

The first image will serve as the "thumbnail" image that shoppers will see in Etsy searches. So use your best overall picture first, since it will have the most exposure, and must do the best job at grabbing the attention of shoppers.

You can rearrange the order of photos by "dragging and dropping" the thumbnails. Depress your computer mouse button on a thumbnail, drag the mouse to scoot the image, then release the mouse button.

To see how an image will appear on the site, click the magnifying-glass icon to view a larger version of the image. If you decide against using an image you've uploaded, click the X icon to delete it.

Etsy Top-level Categories

Accessories
Art
BagsandPurses
BathandBeauty
BooksandZines
Candles
CeramicsandPottery
Children
Clothing
Crochet
DollsandMiniatures
EverythingElse
Furniture
Geekery
Glass
Holidays
Housewares
Jewelry
Knitting
Music
Needlecraft
PaperGoods
Patterns
Pets
PlantsandEdibles
Quilts
Supplies
Toys
Vintage
Weddings
Woodworking

4. Add item information.

Provide a title for your listing. With the allowed 140 characters, use the words that define your item, and what searchers and likely to type in when they're looking for such an item.

You can use up to 140 characters, so use them wisely. The maximum length for an item title is 140 characters, and you can use symbols like these: / . , ( ) - % & '. You're allowed to capitalize three entire words, but the rest must contain upper-case and lower-case letters. (If you discover you've made a mistake on a listing, you can edit it later by visiting Your Account > Currently For Sale. Click Edit, make your revision, proceed to "Step 5," and click Finish.)

You can use both upper-case and lower-case letters in your item titles.

5. Provide a description (and more). Here you'll explain how you crafted the item, its materials, features, and the size or color.

Your item description can be more than a list of facts. It can be a tale of how and why you created it. Try telling a story—how you learned to craft, the technique you used with the piece, who taught you your skills. If you want shoppers to fall in love and buy your items, you must explain why *you* love them.

Emphasize the quality of materials and craftsmanship. And shoppers want more than a rundown of features, they want to hear benefits—what will the item do for *them*? For example, if you're selling a handmade coffee mug, don't forget to mention, "You'll savor your morning coffee for years to come in this unique mug." Or, "This slinky mermaid costume will make you the center of attention at every party."

Finally, you can optionally add "attributes" to your listing such as recipient, occasion and styles. Who is it made for? What is the texture? If your item suits any occasion or anyone, you needn't select a recipient or occasion. You can add a custom style if none of the styles suits your item.

5. Tag your listing. Tags are sorts of keywords that you can assign to your item to help shoppers find it. You can use as many as 13 tags to describe the item's name, style, size, shape, color, material—whatever is the most likely term that shoppers would search for when looking for such an item.

Put yourself in the place of the shopper who'd be delighted to find your item. What words would they use to search for it? Your listing title and description should already contain some of the appropriate tags.

Tags are usually one word, but could be a short combination of words or a phrase such as "belt buckle."

6. List Materials. Here you can indicate the materials or ingredients used to make the item, such as "cowhide leather."

Like tags, the "materials" are words or short descriptive phrases separated by commas.

Shoppers are able to search for (or filter out) materials using Etsy's "Advanced Search" form. Item listings may specify up to 14 materials.

Selling information

Here you'll indicate your item's price, quantity and shipping information.

Price. Your selling price, not including shipping.

Quantity. If you have more than one of the same item, you can indicate how many you have in stock. As items are purchased, the quantity number will decrease.

Because Etsy's basic listing fee is 20 cents, if you list an item for sale with a quantity of five, you'll be charged $1.

Each unique item requires a listing. If you offer an otherwise identical item in pink and blue, you should have two listings, one for each color. This can prevent a lot of confusion among buyers.

Tax. Indicate if you're collecting sales tax. We'll discuss tax requirements and how to configure your Etsy account for this later.

Shipping Info. If you have shipping profiles configured at Etsy, you can select one now from the dropdown menu. Otherwise, you can indicate your shipping fee for this item. You'll indicate what country you're shopping from and which locations you're offering to ship to. You'll state the primary shipping cost for sending the item, and a secondary "with another item" cost to include additional purchases in the same shipment.

Buyers (and Etsy itself) expects sellers' shipping costs to be "reasonable" and not too much more than it actually costs. Sometimes, however, predicting your exact costs is impossible. For example, Etsy sellers can list only one shipping cost per region, like the entire U.S. The problem is, your shipping bill can vary widely, depending on the distance to your customer—especially if the package is heavy. So, many sellers include a statement in their item description or shop policies like this: "I charge **actual** shipping, so if your item costs less to ship than I originally quoted, I will refund you the difference."

Preview and post your listing

After you've completed the information, click the Preview Listing button at the bottom of the page. You'll see how your listing will appear to Etsy shoppers. On the next page you'll see an example of a published listing page.

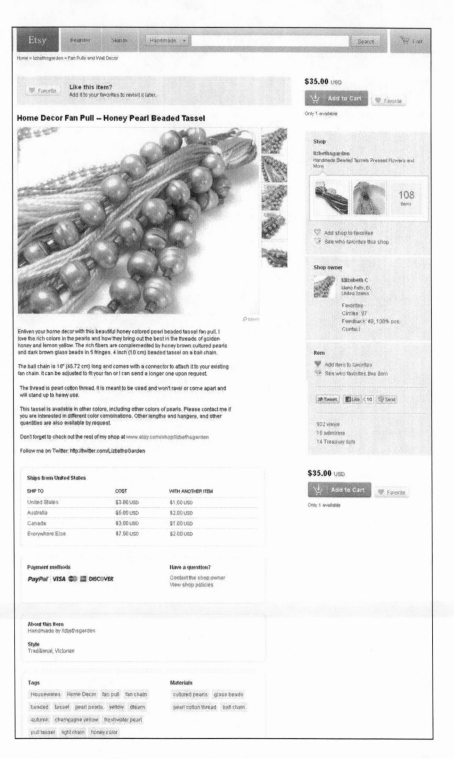

If you notice anything that needs tweaking, click the Edit button and make your changes. If you're not quite ready to make the listing live, or you must leave your computer for a while, click the Save as Draft button. This preserves your work, and you can access it anytime by visiting Your Account > Draft Listings. You won't be charged the listing fee until you publish it.

Drafts never expire, and there is no limit on the number of drafts you may have. The "listed on" date isn't set and you are not charged the listing fee until you click the blue Publish button and add the listing to your shop.

Now your listing is live. It should appear within search results and categories momentarily, although sometimes this can take a few hours.

Editing listings. It's not uncommon to find something you want to change about a listing after you've published it. Simply go to Your Account>Currently for Sale, and click the Edit link on the right. You can also begin editing a listing directly from the listing page. Look on the top of the screen for a row of Listing Tools. You're able to edit any element of the listing, including the text, price, photos, and tags. The item is still available for purchase until you preview and approve the changes. But if you wish, you can deactivate the listing to prevent its purchase until you're finished editing.

Etsy won't charge you for editing a listing, but if you increase the quantity in stock, you'll be charged 20 cents for each unit you add.

Made-to-order, custom items

In Etsy's handmade categories, sellers can offer customized items. You create such listings by selecting Made to Order in response to the prompt, When did you make it?

Some special rules apply to custom items:

- Customizable items must be listed at a set price. If you offer different styles or sizes that affect the price, create a separate listing for each.

- If you use photographs of previous work to illustrate your item, explain in your listing that it's merely an example. Buyers must purchase the listing to have the item made. Discuss the details through email or Convos.

Shops also may solicit buyers who want to request custom handmade items. Advertise this option by putting a link in your shop for Request Custom Item by visiting Your Account > Options, then enable Request Custom Item. Work out the details with the customer, then create a listing for them to purchase.

Reserving a listing for a buyer. If you're creating a listing for a specific buyer, it's prudent to indicate its "reserved" status. There's no automatic way to prohibit other shoppers from buying it, so in your listing title you should indicate the item is "Reserved" for "User name." You can also edit an existing item listing to indicate to other Etsians that an item is already reserved.

What if the buyer for whom the listing is reserved doesn't purchase promptly? You may remove the "Reserved" designation whenever you like. However, you should explain your policy on this to customers, and post an explanation in your Policies page.

Find the listing ID for your item

Each listing has a unique code called a "listing ID number." You'll need the number to add the listing to a Showcase.

The listing ID appears in the Web address on the item's page. Also, the listing ID number is displayed on the item listing page in the right sidebar.

Listing IDs don't appear on sold items. After the purchase, the listing ID is replaced by a transaction ID.

Copy your listings

If you're listing similar items or continually reuse certain information in your descriptions, the "Copy" function can be a tremendous time-saver. Instead of retyping or entering the same information, copy the listing and edit it as needed.

You may use two methods to copy listings:

• Visit Your Account > Currently for Sale to copy active listings. For sold items, visit Sold Orders. Locate the listing, and click Copy.

• Copy a listing directly from your shop or transaction page. While you're signed into your account, a row of listing tools will appear across the top. Click the link for Copy.

You'll arrive at Step 1 of the listing process described above. The form is prefilled with the information from the copied listing. Edit as needed, review and publish.

The copied listing will appear on a new Web page with a new listing ID. Views and hearts from the original listing don't transfer to the new listing.

Renewing your sold listings

An alternative to Etsy's "Copy" function is your ability to "Renew" listings. The advantage here is that page views and hearts carry over. Let's say you're creating an item identical to one that you've previously sold. Renewing the listing will put it back in your shop, while preserving the Web address, hearts, and view counts. As a result, shoppers who might already have the link to your item, or have marked it a favorite, can easily return to the listing and buy it.

To renew sold items, visit Your Account > Sold Orders > Completed. Under the item title is a link for Renew. Click the link, and confirm the renewal.

You can renew sold listings directly from the transaction page in the public view of your shop. Click the Renew link at the top of the page, then confirm the renewal.

Renewed listings appear with a new "listed-on" date, and expire 120 days later.

Deactivate your listings

Let's imagine you want to make an item unavailable for sale for a while. Perhaps you have decided to replace the listing's images, or you're attending a show and may sell some items. Instead of deleting the listings, simply "deactivate" the listings temporarily.

To deactivate a listing, visit Your Account > Currently For Sale. On the left of each item listing, there's a checkbox you can click. Then click the Deactivate button at the top or bottom of the page.

To reactivate a listing, visit Your Account > Inactive Listings. Click the checkbox next to the desired item, then click Activate. If you need to change any details about the listing, click Edit to the right of the listing.

No fee is charged when you reactivate a listing. Inactive listings don't appear on Etsy's public site, but the period of inactivity still counts as part of the four-month listing duration.

Listing expirations

For the 20-cent listing fee, your listings appear for 120 days before expiring. To monitor the expiration dates of your listings, visit Your Account > Currently For Sale. You'll see a column of expiration dates, and you can sort the column by date by clicking the word Expires at the top.

You can renew an expired listing by visiting Your Account > Expired List-ings. Click the checkbox next to the desired items, then click Renew at the top or bottom of the page.

Delete a listing

To remove a listing from your shop, visit Your Account > Currently For Sale. Locate the item listing you wish to remove and click on the box to the left of it. Then click on Delete at the top of the page. No fee is charged to delete a listing, and you receive no refund for the original listing fee. Remember that once you delete a listing, you won't be able to retrieve the information any-more. To preserve the data in the listing, simply inactivate the listing.

SELLER PROFILE: Angie's Suds 'N Such

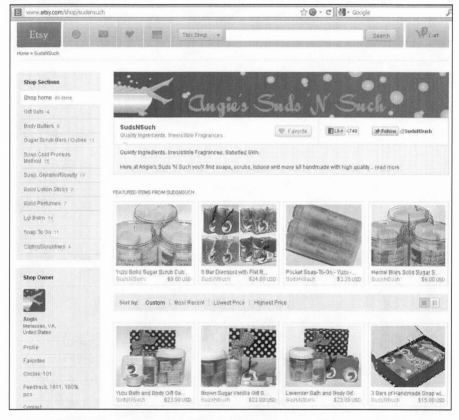

Angie Barrett of Manassas, Va., grew her soap making hobby into a full-fledged Etsy business. She uses tiered pricing, including in her featured items low-priced pocket soap alongside two fancier, more expensive collections.
See **Etsy.com/shop/sudsnsuch**.

How did you get started?

It started as a hobby. Every year I'd make something to give out to family members along with their Christmas gifts. One year, I decided to make soap. Everyone loved it, and kept telling me I should sell it.

So, I started building up stock for craft shows, and in the meantime found Etsy. I've been selling on Etsy ever since.

What's your creative process?

A lot of my soap ideas come from food—I make soap in the shape of pizza, ice cream sandwiches, and popcorn. It comes from my love of baking. I'll browse through a cookbook, see some new dessert, and think, "That would make a great soap!"

How has your business evolved since you started, and how has the economy affected things?

In the beginning, my business was a hobby. I was doing daycare full-time, and never really considered my soap making to be a "business." When we moved to a new home, I decided that soap making was what I wanted to do full-time. So I started working harder, promoting more, doing more craft shows, and gaining more wholesale accounts.

Herbal Bliss Solid Sugar Scrub Cubes

Want a delicious way to have beautiful skin? These solid sugar scrubs are perfect!

Made with pure cane sugar to exfoliate while the glycerin soap provides a wonderful lather. Once or twice a week while showering, simply crush a scrub in your hand with a small amount of water. Massage gently over your skin. Rinse and towel dry. Voila! Now your skin will feel and smell fantastic!

I've had some slow months during the tough economy, but I use that time to produce new products and to think of new ways to get my name out there.

How do you attract customers and get repeat business?

Finding customers is one of the hardest parts. Fortunately Etsy does a great job of bringing people to me through their search engine. I also have a Facebook page, a blog, and accounts at Twitter and Flickr, which allows customers and potential customers to see my new products and promotions.

Craft shows are a great way to gain local customers, as well as gifting my items. For example, I've received many new customers by giving my items as gifts to my child's teachers and coaches.

What percentage of your sales is online?

About 90 percent of my business is done online through Etsy. The other 10 percent is mostly craft shows.

What's your procedure for pricing your items?

I base my prices on my cost of supplies, Etsy and PayPal fees, and the amount of time required to make the item. I also factor in wholesale. My prices need to be high enough so I can offer a decent discount to wholesalers, but not so high that the price discourages retail sales.

PHOTOGRAPH YOUR ITEMS LIKE A PRO

Selling on Etsy has tremendous advantages over traditional craft selling, which demands shelf space, travel, fair booth rentals, and so forth. Instead of being limited to one geographical area, you're potentially selling to the whole world. The big disadvantage at Etsy is your customer can't personally see and inspect your item. You've got to make up for it by taking great photographs.

Would you spend much money on something if you weren't sure what it looked like? Of course not. So, if you don't provide four or five excellent illustrations of your item, shoppers may wonder whether you really have the item in stock, how professional it is, or if you're hiding some horrible defect.

If you don't already use a digital camera, now is the time to get one and learn to use it. Popular cameras such as the Sony Cyber-Shot, priced at about $100, have all the necessary features for most product photography. You can probably find a recent used model at a significant discount.

Can you get by with photos you've taken with a cellphone? It depends on the optics of your phone and the size of your item. Small items, like jewelry, require a camera with a "macro" setting which enables you to take extreme close-up shots illustrating fine detail or texture. On your camera viewfinder, the macro feature is usually represented by a tulip icon. Most cellphone cameras aren't up to this task.

To make your pictures effective, keep it simple. Focus in closely on the item. Using a piece of poster board or cloth as a backdrop can improve your image, but also give some thought to what kinds of textures and props you might use to highlight your item. Use natural lighting when possible to reduce the shadows that result from a flash, or augment your natural lighting with one or two lamps. A couple of student desktop study lamps can produce adequate lighting.

Good photos will drive traffic to your Etsy shop. Great photos not only sell your product, but they also get attention when curators are choosing items to include in Treasuries. To best showcase your product, photograph it from more than one angle. Be sure to include a closeup and at least one photo that shows the item's scale compared to a familiar prop like a penny or ruler.

You can make your items more desirable by showing them in use in your photos. Rather than a static hat on a hat stand, photograph your creation being worn by your friend's teenage daughter, the one who loves to pose for the camera. If you think your vintage china plate would make a great soap dish, put some pretty soaps in it, and take one photo of it next to a stack of fluffy towels.

For your close-ups, tilt the camera a bit to find the best angle, or focus on the prettiest detail, such as the embossing on a handmade greeting card. Get ideas for pleasing photos by flipping through home and gardening magazines.

Vintage items require special consideration. Your photos should reveal any obvious wear or defects, lest you be accused of concealing them.

You can enhance your product photos for free by using **Picnik.com**. (Photo of "Math Geek Necklace" courtesy of Cathy Stein, Etsy seller EclecticSkeptic.)

Even if your photos aren't perfect, you can clean them up and crop or resize them using Photoshop or the free online tool at Picnik.com. The great thing about Picnik is its basic service is free and easy to learn—you're adjusting your photo right in your computer's Web browser. You can adjust the color and add text to the photo. (Picnik is also a good tool for creating or editing Etsy avatars and Shop banners.) In 2012, Picnik was acquired by Google, and most of its features are still available free. For more information, see http://support.google.com/picnik/?p=googleplus.

Another free online photo editing tool is Photoshop Express, Photoshop.com/tools/overview.

Whatever you do, don't include an "accidental" background in your product shots, like a nearby pile of dirty clothes or dishes—if something doesn't belong in your photo, crop it out. A natural background can work fine, such as a piece of paper, a brick wall, or a bunch of flowers.

Etsy's Web pages require that images be a certain size. If your images are outside the recommended parameters, the site will attempt to resize them, although picture quality will be degraded. Here are the expected sizes for Etsy images:

Avatars: 75x75 pixels.

Shop Banners: 760x100 pixels.

Team Logo: 170x100 pixels.

Listing Images: 570 pixels wide.

How to take great product photos

A picture is worth a thousand clicks—or more. Showing up in search results is one thing, but you've also got to invite people to click and visit your listing. Here's where a great photograph of your listing helps. If a shopper is scanning through a list of search results, they're more likely to click on the listings with eye-catching thumbnail images. Try it yourself and see: Scroll through a list of Etsy search results. You'll naturally gravitate toward the ones with a good photo.

Anyone can take a simple snapshot of an item with an automatic camera and get acceptable results. But special care is required to make a static object look its best, and make shoppers notice and want the featured item. That doesn't mean an amateur photographer can't do a great job. It just means you need to understand the available tools and master a few simple techniques, according to my photographer friend, who goes by the name Camera Jim. Here are his tips for taking great product photos:

- **Use natural light.** If you had to choose just one light to use for product photography, it should be the light coming from a bright window without direct sunlight. That's because this light is both large (which is what makes it diffuse and soft) and it is directional, which can help show off the shape and texture of your subject.

• **Use a tripod for sharp photos.** A solid support for your camera is another important tool because it prevents blurring due to camera motion. Most "out of focus" shots aren't really unfocused. They're blurry because the camera moved slightly during exposure.

• **Create a second light with a reflector.** Add light to brighten or fill shadows on the other side of the subject. Your fill light can be simply a flat piece of light-colored poster board, propped up and used as a reflector. This controls the highlight and shadow values in your scene. If the main light is too strong in relation to the fill light, the highlights will be washed out and the shadows will be too dark. If the fill light is too strong, you might wipe out the shadows completely and lose the sense of shape they give your subject. Fortunately, digital cameras allow an immediate review of your results, so you can easily experiment with your fill light.

• **Use basic artificial light.** If you don't have a handy window or you need to shoot at night, you can use plain old tungsten (incandescent) lights. These are regular household bulbs, the kind you use in table lamps. Two 150-watt bulbs are enough, as long as you remember to use that tripod. You can use these bulbs in photographic reflectors with light stands (available on eBay or from a camera shop) or simple clamp-on reflectors of the sort sold at home centers for $10 or less. For best results, preset your camera's "white balance" control to "tungsten" or "incandescent." If you're using compact fluorescent bulbs for lighting, take an extra step to ensure color accuracy: consult your camera's manual for setting a custom white balance.

• **Diffuse lights for window-like softness.** You can turn those artificial lights into soft, window-like sources by aiming them through translucent white material (a sheet of tracing paper, a piece of white plastic, etc.) or by bouncing them off reflectors.

• **Use a model.** Especially for clothing, jewelry and certain accessories, include some shots with a live model wearing or using your item. When shoppers see your item displayed with a model, they can more easily imagine themselves wearing or using it, and will be more likely to buy it.

• **Use a light tent.** This lighting tool is used often by professional product photographers, and commercially made light tents have become popular with Etsy sellers. Search on Etsy, eBay or Amazon for "light tent" and you'll find hundreds for sale. These small, white, cube-shaped tents have one open side where you insert your camera lens.

- **Use the "milk jug" light tent.** The simplest and cheapest form of a light tent for small objects is a plastic milk jug with the bottom cut off.

The white plastic diffuses the light inside the jug. Shoot through the neck or a hole cut in the side.

For medium-sized items, this tabletop photo tent by Idirectmart enables good product photography. It's available for about $30 at Amazon.com.

Jewelry photography with a light tent

Jewelry can be dazzling, but it's one of the most difficult items to photograph well. On one small item, you can have many different surfaces such as smooth gold or silver, faceted gems, and even textured engraving or filigree. Each surface reflects and refracts light differently. And, since light is what we're capturing when we take a photo, how we light each item determines how the final image will appear.

For an item such as a gold necklace, using a small light tent usually allows you to capture fine detail without glare spots, which detract from your image.

An item like a watch has special lighting needs because of the flat face of the crystal, which can reflect light and obscure the dial. In such a case, try inserting a small spot of black paper inside your light tent, so that would be the area reflected by the crystal.

When editing jewelry photos on your computer, try increasing the "sharpness" setting in order to bring out the fire and sparkle of the stones.

For more photography tutorials, see Camerajim.com.

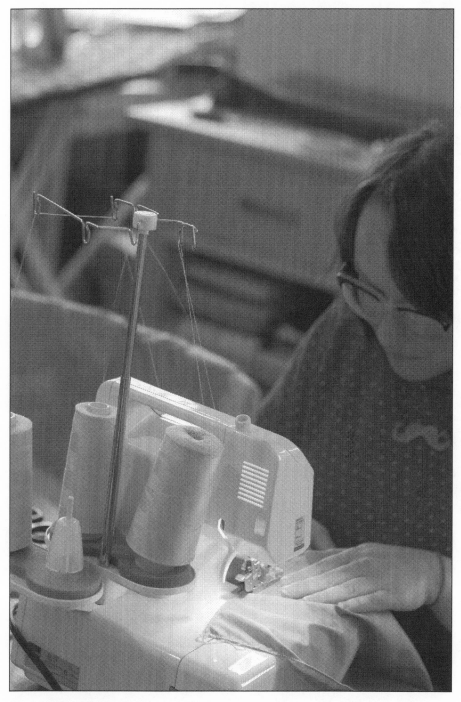

Sewing at the Etsy lab in Brooklyn, New York.

ORGANIZE AND MANAGE YOUR SHOP

Now our Etsy shop is up and running, but we've got several more tasks ahead to ensure we're humming at full speed.

Organize your shop into sections. Once you've got several different items for sale, organize your shop into sections, which will be displayed as links in your shop's sidebar. This is a no-brainer: Dividing your shop into sections helps you stay organized, and helps your shopper browse and find what they're looking for faster.

Using sections, you can group listings in a variety of ways, like a brick-and-mortar department store. Or your sections might pertain to sizes, types of construction, or product line. You're allowed up to 10 shop sections, plus a link for All Items, which appears by default.

To add or edit your shop sections, visit Your Account > Info & Appearance > Sections. Click Create a new section, type in the title of the section, up to 24 characters, then click Save. You can delete a section by clicking the trash-can icon, but this does not deactivate any existing listings—they merely won't appear in that section anymore. Instead, they'll appear only in All Items. You can put a listing in only one section.

To change the order of your sections, drag the move icon for that section while holding your computer mouse.

Once you've established your shop sections, you'll be able to assign new items to the correct section during the listing process. You won't have to "rearrange" your store again unless, perhaps, you add new types of merchandise to your shop.

However you designate your shop's sections, they aren't necessarily connected to Etsy's site-wide "categories." Nor are your shop sections related to listing tags.

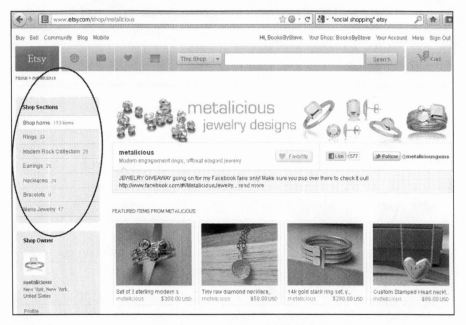

Shop sections, shown in the left sidebar, enable customers to easily navigate your store.

Change the order of your shop listings

You might want to move your most popular or profitable items to a more prominent spot using the Rearrange Your Shop tool. Using your computer mouse, click and drag your item listings to change the order on your item pages. You can also change the page on which items appear.

To rearrange your shop:

1. Visit Your Account > Options. At the top of the page is a section labeled Rearrange Your Shop. Click the button beside Enabled.

2. Make your changes, then check the public view of your shop by clicking the Shop icon in the navigation bar near the top.

3. When you're finished rearranging, click Save Changes.

4. While you're signed into Etsy, you'll also see a link in the sidebar of your shop, Rearrange Your Shop.

5. After rearranging your shop, when you add a new listing or renew an old one, the new listing automatically appears first. So if you want a new listing to appear in a different spot, you'll need to rearrange the shop again.

Visit **Your Shop > Options** to rearrange listings.

Feature your items

In your Etsy shop you can feature as many as four listings atop your home page, below the Shop Announcement. To feature items, visit Your Account>Currently For Sale, and click the star icon beside each listing you want to feature. If you select more than four items and a featured item sells out, the next item on your list appears. If you don't select any items to be featured, this space on your shop's home page appears blank.

You can adjust the ranking of the featured listings to determine the order in which they appear. Visit Your Account > Featured Listings.

Collect payments

Since PayPal is the most popular online payment service for independent online merchants, having a PayPal business account is practically a must for Etsy sellers. You must open an account at PayPal if you want to accept it as a form of payment at your Etsy shop. If you already have a PayPal account, it's fairly easy to upgrade the account to "premier" or "business" status. Upgrading your account will enable you to use PayPal's service to accept payments from anyone using a credit card, regardless of whether they have an account with PayPal. Another advantage of premier and business PayPal accounts is that there's no ceiling on transactions—as an anti-fraud measure, personal PayPal accounts may accept no more than $500 in payments per month.

Send PayPal invoices directly to buyers

Occasionally you'll need to send a PayPal invoice to your buyer. Perhaps the buyer was confused about how to complete the transaction, or perhaps this is an order for which you require a deposit, or you've reduced the shipping fees.

To create the PayPal invoice:

- Log into PayPal.com and click Request Money.

- Click Create Invoice.

- In drop-down menu, select New Invoice and Continue.

On this page you'll enter the following information, which also appears on the Etsy invoice at Your Account > Sold Orders:

1. Email address for buyer
2. Item quantity
3. Etsy transaction ID (appears on PayPal invoice as Item ID)
4. Item title
5. Item price
6. Shipping cost

- When prompted for the Invoice Type, select Goods.

- When you've finished entering all the information, press Continue.

- Double-check all your entries on the invoice, and click Send Invoice. Your buyer will receive an email from PayPal with instructions on completing the payment. Until the buyer pays, the invoice will appear as "pending" in your Etsy account.

PayPal enables you to save a template of the invoice after sending it, which can be a time-saver if you will process similar transactions in the future.

Canceling orders or transactions

If you don't receive the payment within a few days, you might send a courteous reminder to your buyer. If you don't receive a response, which happens occasionally, you can cancel the order and renew the listing.

To contact your buyer, get the email address in the sales email Etsy sends for each sale. You can also view the buyer's user name from the invoice page, then send a message via Conversations.

You'll find the transaction invoice at Your Account > Sold Orders. Click the invoice link beside the item listing.

To cancel an order or transaction, visit Your Account > Sold Orders. Click the invoice link for the related order. In the "Order" section on this page, click Cancel a transaction. Etsy should process the cancellation within two days.

Canceling a transaction deletes the record from your account.

Cancel part of an order

A single Etsy order may contain multiple "transactions" because each item within an order is classified as a unique transaction with its own transaction ID number. You can cancel all, or some, transactions in an order.

Once Etsy finishes processing the cancellation, you'll no longer have the ability to leave feedback. Also, your listing description and images will be deleted after the cancellation is finalized, so if you want to reuse them, renew the item before canceling the transaction.

Download your listings and transaction records

You can download your existing Etsy listings in a text file viewable in a spreadsheet program such as Microsoft Excel, Google Spreadsheets, or OpenOffice Calc. This enables you to quickly sort through a lot of data, or analyze the prices and quantities associated with your listings. If you use an accounting program such as Intuit QuickBooks, you can import this data there.

To download a file of your listings, visit Your Account > Options and click the tab for Download Data. Click Download CSV to save the text file to your computer.

To download records of your sales, visit Your Account > Sold Orders. Select the desired month and year from the menu at the top. Click Go. At the bottom of the page, click Download Orders to save the file.

Locate orders from your shop

You can access your sold orders in Your Account > Sold Orders. Select the available tabs to view open, completed, or "all" orders. You can also search by various criteria:

- listing title

- buyer name

- message from buyer

- buyer user name

- ship to name or address

- receipt id

- transaction id

You can sort your list of orders according to most recent, oldest, and total value.

Collect sales tax

Etsy doesn't provide any advice to members regarding sales taxes. It's up to you to research local laws on how to collect and report the applicable sales taxes. It all depends on the rules in your state and local government.

In most U.S. states, current rules generally require "remote" sellers (operating via Internet, telephone or mail-order, instead of a walk-on store) to collect applicable state and local sales taxes. Current practice is that sellers collect tax on sales shipped to buyers in their home state, but not on out-of-state sales.

If you need to collect tax on certain purchases through your shop, you can use Etsy's Sales Tax settings to apply tax to the required states, Canadian province, or country.

To automatically collect the required state sales tax on Etsy, visit Your Account > Shop Settings > Shipping & Payment. Enter the required U.S. state, percentages, and ZIP Codes.

Automate your business with apps and software

In the section about shipping, we learned how to save time and tedium by using PayPal to automatically print shipping labels and postage. Several more tools are available for sellers who want to automate some of their administrative chores. Some of these tools, called applications or apps, are absolutely free, while some require a monthly subscription fee.

One caveat about Etsy apps: Most of them are provided by an independent developer, not Etsy itself. So Etsy doesn't guarantee that these apps work as advertised. Another possibility is that Etsy will update its system design, throwing one or more of these apps out of whack, at least temporarily.

This is just a sampling of the dozens of Etsy apps available. An updated list is available at Etsy.com/apps/shop_tools.

With those caveats in mind, here are some of the more popular:

Betsi. A listing-management and bulk editing tool for Etsy sellers. Filter listings according to section, category, tag, or material, then choose from 18 actions, including add, replace, delete, reorder tags and/or materials, change titles, pricing, categories, sections, renew, relist. Drag and drop for quick operation.

Stitch Labs. Automates orders and relisting. A centralized inventory management system considers different ways you might sell—Etsy, wholesale, consignment, trunk shows—so that all your sales information is in one place and you can analyze your business. Stitch can generate invoices, packing slips and line sheets, and help you track expenses.

CraftLaunch. Automatically showcases your Etsy shop listings in a customized, branded website. You can complement selling with storytelling to build your brand, add your company history, and provide show dates and wholesale information

Etsy for iPhone. Unlike the apps mentioned above from independent developers, this one is from Etsy's in-house staff. As a buyer, you can search for items, browse Treasury Lists, and make purchases from your phone. As a seller, you can access your listings and latest orders, and use merchant tools to manage your business away from your computer.

Craftopolis.com. Craftopolis offers a variety of tools for shop owners. One gives sellers access to their sales data, hearts, views and alerts of upcoming expiring listings in an easy-to-understand calendar format. Second, a batch editing tool provides a convenient way to edit prices, titles, descriptions, and item quantities. You can edit individual listings, whole sections, or your entire shop in just a few clicks. Third, a tag report shows what search terms people are using to find your items through Etsy search, providing insight into which tags are working for you, and which are under-performing.

Craftlaunch.com. CraftLaunch is a tool for easily displaying your Etsy listings on your own fully branded website. You can complement selling with storytelling to build your brand. Add your company history, show dates, wholesale information, news, and more.

Outright.com is a free and simple way for Etsy sellers to automate their bookkeeping chores.

Take a vacation

If you plan to be away from your business and unable to ship orders, you should put your shop "on vacation." This account setting removes your item listings from public view. If you're unable to handle customers promptly, it's much better to put things on hold for a few days, rather than risk appearing inattentive. Should you have a friend or family member mind your shop while you're away? Well, remember that you'll be held directly responsible for whatever happens with your account, and that you've promised that shipments will be handled under your direct supervision.

To put your shop on or off Vacation Mode, visit Your Shop > Options > Vacation Mode. Make your selection, On or Off, then click Save. (The Options link is in the Shop Settings section on the left column of Your Shop. Vacation Mode is the second tab at the top of this page.)

You won't be able to edit or create new listings while your account is on vacation, but your Favorites still appear. You should enter a brief message on your Shop Announcement to explain you're away, and when you'll return. While your shop is on vacation, members can sign up to receive an email notice when you're open for business again.

Another idea: write an auto-response message in the event you get a Convo while you're away. Once you activate vacation mode, you'll see the option to write an automatic message.

While your shop is on vacation, your items can't be purchased. Listings generally are visible—they won't appear in searches—but they appear in Favorites and Treasuries. For people who click a link to a listing from outside Etsy, they'll see the listing page along with a notice that you're away.

An alternative to Etsy's vacation mode is simply making your listings inactive for a while. Sometimes Etsians will do this if they don't want to advertise that they're out of town. To inactivate your listings, visit Your Account > Currently for Sale. Click the checkboxes next to all the listings you want to idle. When you're ready for business again, reactivate your listings by visiting Your Account > Inactive listings.

SELLER PROFILE: Purple and Lime

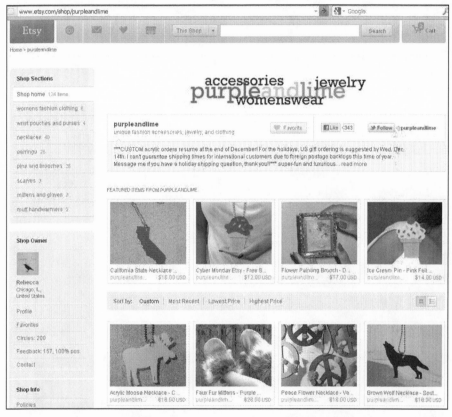

Rebecca George, proprietor of Purple and Lime, specializes in jewelry, womenswear, and accessories "that make you smile." Working from Chicago, she sells her designs on Etsy, at shows, and has her own website for wholesale orders.

See **Etsy.com/shop/purpleandlime**.

How did you get started?

I moved back to the United States after attending fashion school in London, then held many office jobs that didn't make me happy. I've always wanted my own clothing and accessories line, so I opened an Etsy shop. Since I was a child I have drawn and created fashion!

My Etsy shop has super-fun women's clothing, jewelry, and accessories. I love making people smile with colorful, quirky themes and textures. I enjoy the whole process of listing, selling, packing up orders, and even taking them to the Post Office. But the best feeling is getting a nice email or feedback from a happy customer.

How has your business evolved since then?

Several ways: Diversifying through teaching and Etsy coaching, creating different products I never would have expected to make, like mittens, and selling in some unique places and shows, like plays.

The teaching has been really exciting. I love sharing Etsy tips that I wish I'd known when I started.

What's your best advice for newbies?

Don't be afraid to ask other artists and business owners for advice. And then, pass that advice along!

Where do you get ideas?

My creative process varies. Sometimes I start with a completely new idea and test it out, and other times my pieces develop organically from another item I already make. When crafting handmade items, the most important thing is to put a little love in each product.

My niche is catering to women who love fun and color. My customers say that my work has a sense of humor. For example, despite being vegetarian, I'll use imagery of bacon and other breakfast items because I love iconographic, bold pop art, like Warhol. I find it very humorous.

How do you find customers and repeat business?

I attract customers to my Etsy shop through social networking—Facebook, Twitter—and by meeting people while wearing my products, and through word of mouth.

Providing exceptional customer service brings people back to my shop. That's one of the best things about selling on Etsy—you are able to communicate directly with your customer and work with them to create the best shopping experience possible.

What proportion of your business is online, offline and shows?

My sales are approximately 70 percent Etsy, 20 percent craft shows, and 10 percent consignment. My products are definitely seasonal, as I love making winter accessories and outerwear. So the bulk of my business is in the fall and winter. Craft shows are great all year round, especially before holidays, because people love to see and touch products in person.

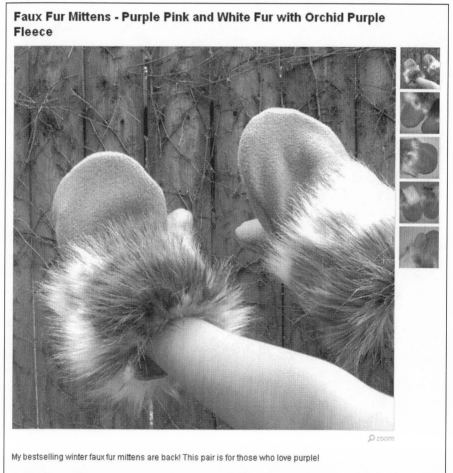

Faux Fur Mittens - Purple Pink and White Fur with Orchid Purple Fleece

My bestselling winter faux fur mittens are back! This pair is for those who love purple!

- made from wonderful orchid purple no-pill fleece with white/purple/dark pink fake fur trim around the wrist

How do you price your items?

I have a formula, and also evaluate competitors' pricing to determine my retail prices.

SHIP YOUR TREASURES

Shipping is a critical phase of your business, and a frequent source of friction with customers. For many sellers, shipping is one of the least-fun parts of doing business online. Compared with crafting, shipping can be a dreadful chore. But it's just as critical to your success. You can have the world's best products and the best intentions in the world, but if you ship your items late or don't keep customers informed, it creates headaches that can snowball.

Small problems turn into large problems unless you're fanatical about shipping. If you allow problems to fester, you'll suffer from customer complaints, nasty feedback, and time-consuming research in response to customer inquiries, like "Where's my package?"

Get organized. Have a routine and stick with it, and you'll keep customers happy and have plenty of time to do the parts of your business you enjoy more. Shipping sold items the following morning is a good habit. At a minimum, you should ship twice a week.

Etsy leaves sellers a lot of leeway on fulfillment and shipping. They have to, because shops are so vastly different—located potentially anywhere in the world, selling a multitude of products, and with a wide variety of shipping carriers available. As a result, getting the shipping settings just right on your Etsy seller account is somewhat complicated, and requires some thought.

Processing orders and shipping

When one of your items sells, you'll receive an email from Etsy including all the transaction details—the item, buyer, shipping address, payment method, and so on. The same transaction details will appear under Your Account > Sold Orders.

After you've received payment, ship the item to your customer. Ensure the funds appear in your PayPal account or, in the case of checks and money orders, wait for the payment to arrive in the mail and be cleared by your bank.

Under Sold Orders, the Open tab will show which orders are awaiting shipment. After you mark it "shipped," the transaction will move to the Completed tab. (If you accidentally mark an order "completed," you can move it back to the Open tab.)After the transaction is complete, leave your buyer feedback at Your Account > Feedback > Items Awaiting Feedback.

Depending upon the shipping service, you might calculate your shipping rates by weight, or by volume. For example, if you're selling small, light-weight items like earrings, USPS First Class Mail may be your best option. If you're selling relatively compact, heavy items, perhaps a USPS Flat Rate Priority Box would make sense. Larger, heavier items might go best with the USPS Parcel rate—or, if that's too slow, maybe UPS, United Parcel Service.

The holiday buying season can be one of your most lucrative parts of the year, but be sure to announce order deadlines to prevent disappointed customers. For example, you might ask customers to order before Dec. 15 to ensure delivery by Christmas.

Expedited shipping. As the old saying goes, the best things are worth waiting for. Unfortunately, a growing percentage of online shoppers aren't content to wait, not even a few days. These folks demand overnight shipping, and offering it can close a sale for you -- or lose a sale if it's not an option. You'll need to calculate your costs for overnight delivery of each of your items, and decide if it makes sense to offer overnight shipping.

Here's a good way to handle express shipping: Let customers know whether you offer it, how much extra you charge for it, and instructions on how to request it. Many sellers simply state something like this in the Shop Announcement or Policy Page:

> *Express shipping costs $8 extra. If you*
> *want this service, please request it in the*
> *"Message to Seller" box at checkout, and I'll*
> *send you a revised PayPal invoice for the*
> *added cost.*

Shipping through PayPal

If you use the Postal Service as your primary shipping carrier, you can co-ordinate your shipping using PayPal, even for customers who paid using another method. PayPal's shipping service enables you to print prepaid shipping labels, without service fees, for use with the U.S. Postal Service, UPS, Canada Post, or U.K. Royal Mail. For international packages, if you can afford the higher-priced Priority Mail International rate, PayPal preprints the customs forms, which saves you the tedium of completing the forms by hand. Another option is to use the Postal Service's Web site, Usps.com, which has a handy template for complete your customs forms.

While we're on the subject of customs forms, be aware that some overseas customers will ask you to mark their item as a "gift" instead of merchandise, so they can avoid required customs fees. Don't do it. Your item might be delayed by customs officials, especially if the package contains an invoice.

If you're a new seller, you might consider international shipping only to Canada, Mexico and European Union countries for a while. For U.S. sellers, these nations provide the bulk of overseas business, anyway. After you're more accustomed to international shipping, you can expend into more territories.

To ship through PayPal:

• Log into your account at PayPal.com and click the Merchant Services tab.

• Click the Shipping Preferences link under Shipping & Tax.

• Under Default Shipping Carrier, click U.S. Postal Service (the other option is UPS). Click Save.

• Now you'll be able to print shipping labels and postage for each Pay-Pal payment received by visiting the Payments Received section of your PayPal account and clicking the Print Shipping Label link beside each transaction. To ship items paid for outside PayPal, visit this address: Paypal.com/us/cgi-bin/webscr?cmd=_ship-now, and enter the shipping name and address.

PayPal multiorder shipping tool. If you have a batch of orders to send simultaneously, PayPal's multi-order tool is a great time-saver. It automatically imports your paid Etsy orders when you launch it, and you can preset the terms for frequently shipped items. After you've printed your labels, you can arrange a USPS pickup from the multi-order screen, and save yourself a trip to the Post Office.

To use this tool, follow the same steps as above, but instead of clicking Print Shipping Label, click the PayPal Multi-order Shipping link.

Save time with shipping profiles

The shipping profile feature lets you save a template of shipping information to be quickly applied to any of your items while listing or editing. Shipping profiles work best if you sell several items that are about the same size and weight. You'll save time by pre-calculating your shipping costs for packages of certain sizes.

To create or edit a shipping profile, visit Your Account>Shipping & Payment>Shipping Profiles. Click Create a New Profile, and give it a name, such as "Small Priority Box." Indicate the country from which the package is being shipped and its destination country. Then add these costs: the "primary ship-ping costs," (your fee to ship this item alone), and the "secondary shipping costs," which is usually an incremental shipping fee to cover adding another item to the package.

After you've created shipping profiles, you can use them while listing new items, or insert them into existing listings using Etsy's batch shipping tool mentioned in the next section. If you edit a shipping profile to change its terms, you'll need to reapply it to existing listings if you want the changes to apply to those listings; they won't update automatically.

Batch shipping tool. This feature works much like the "sections" fea-ture, which allows you to assign sections to a list of your items in one fell swoop.

First, you'll need to have some shipping profiles. Then you can batch as-sign them to your items. Here's the procedure:

1. Click the Batch Shipping link under the Items link in your account.

2. You'll see a list of all currently listed items with a box next to each. The box is where you'll assign a shipping profile.

3. Select your shipping profile from the drop-down menu next to each item you want to edit.

4. Click the Save Changes button at the top right of the screen.

Combined shipping. This enables you to indicate a special shipping rate in case a buyer purchases multiple items at the same time. Instead of being socked twice by full shipping fees for a purchase that can be shipped in the same package, the buyer pays a bit extra to cover the additional cost.

To offer combined shipping on your listings, you must enter two things: a "primary" shipping fee for shipping the item alone, and a "secondary" ship-ping fee when two or more are shipped together. For example, on a small USPS Priority Box, you might enter $8 for primary shipping, and $2 for sec-ondary shipping. The big discount for shipping on the second item encourages customers to buy more than one item. Some sellers even take this a step further, offering "free" shipping with the second item. To do this, you'd enter $8 for primary shipping and $0.00 for secondary shipping.

Buyers expect to get a break on combined shipping for most items, but you might not want to offer combined shipping on oversized, heavy items that can't be shipped in the same container. In such cases, to avoid offering a discounted shipping fee on the second item, you can enter the same cost for the primary and secondary shipping fees.

International and "everywhere else." You can specify dozens of destination countries and calculate a different shipping fee for each, or you can simply use the flat-rate "Everywhere Else" option. Instead of setting a shipping cost for each country, you'd offer a set fee for those countries where you don't specify a different shipping fee.

Conflicts with PayPal invoices. Like Etsy, PayPal allows sellers to establish shipping profiles. If you've made certain settings in your PayPal account to add shipping fees automatically, you'll need to disable this PayPal feature as described below. Otherwise, the Etsy and PayPal settings will conflict, and your buyers might get double-billed for shipping.

To change your PayPal settings, here's the procedure:

1. To change your PayPal settings, visit PayPal.com > My Account>Profile>Shipping calculations (this appears in the Selling Preferences Column).

2. To change the PayPal shipping calculator, click Start if this is your first time adjusting the calculator. (Or, if you've previously already established a shipping calculator, click Edit.)

3. Select the U.S. states you ship to, and click Continue. In the section labeled What are the shipping rates based on, select Total Order Amount. Click Use the shipping fee based on order amount instead of my calculator's settings, then click Save Changes.

4. If you've already had a PayPal invoice go through with an incorrect shipping address, log into your PayPal account and click request money to send a revised invoice to your buyer.

Regional Shipping. You can set one shipping cost for multiple countries in a group you determine. For example, if you're in the United States, you might discover that it costs you about the same to ship your items to Canada or Mexico. If so, you might establish a "regional shipping" rate to cover these North American countries outside the United States. Likewise, you might establish a regional rate for all locations in the European Union. You can establish primary and secondary rates for each region, just as you can for specific countries.

If necessary, you could establish a Country-Specific Shipping cost for certain countries within your regional shipping zones, and that rate would override the shipping rate established for the region. For example, if you lived in Italy, you'd probably want to set a Country-Specific shipping rate for Italy, and a different rate for farther destinations in the rest of the European Union.

International shipping. Offering international shipping opens the entire world to your business. But, of course, it brings some added complications. Postage and rates are higher, and packages might be subject to customs duties and taxes. You'll need to explain this on your shop's Policies page.

Customs forms enable destination countries to allow the entry of mail without opening each piece for inspection. You can pick up blank copies of these forms at your local Post Office.

Resolve nondelivery disputes

If a buyer claims they haven't received an item you shipped, try to resolve it directly with the buyer using email or a Convo. Often, a prompt response and providing a tracking number, if available, will reassure an impatient buyer who hasn't received their package.

If the buyer files a nondelivery case with Etsy, you'll receive an email detailing the case, and directions on how to resolve it.

To ask a buyer for a "case closure," locate the case by visiting Your Account>Reported Cases. Check the Request closure box and enter a reason for the closure request. Buyers have 7 days to respond before automatic closure.

You should respond promptly to all nondelivery cases to keep your Etsy account in the clear.

What if the case remains open? It will escalate each week, and if it's unresolved after several weeks, your shipping privileges can be suspended.

Certificate of mailing. Every once in a while, it happens. A customer claims not to have received a USPS package, even when a Delivery Confirmation number showed that delivery occurred. Mistakes and theft sometimes occur. One ironclad method of proving you shipped an item is purchasing a "Certificate of Mailing" at your local Post Office. Unfortunately, the forms cost $1.15.

Shipping supplies

Part of a well-oiled shipping routine is having a good supply of all the required boxes, tape, and related supplies. When orders roll in, you can't afford to waste time scrounging around for a suitable box and packing material. And you can save time and money by purchasing your shipping supplies from one of the suppliers listed here instead of local office-supply stores such as Staples or Office Depot.

One reliable vendor for shipping supplies is Associated Bag Co. at AssociatedBag.com. They offer competitive pricing and deliver by the next business day at regular UPS ground rates. Another standby is Uline.com, which has a larger selection of items but can be a bit more expensive. Also, Uline's shipping fees are higher, and next-day delivery costs extra. However, if you place an order for a large quantity, Uline will provide a discount and in some cases free delivery. Another good choice is Paper Mart, Papermart.com.

Another option is searching for local shipping suppliers by consulting your Yellow Pages. If you can avoid shipping fees, that could add up to significant savings over time. Let them know you'll be buying often and in quantity, so they'll quote their best prices.

A postage scale is a good investment because you can often ship your packages from home after you've determined the weight and calculated the fees.

Enclose some extras in your packages

Don't forget the details. Do you offer a coupon code for repeat customers? Enclose a small notice about it in your packages. Ensure your customers know about your discount right as they open your package.

A brief note thanking the customer and mentioning them by name is a nice touch. For example, "Thank you, Suzanne, for ordering my crochet beanie. I hope you have as much fun wearing it as I did making it! If you have time, let me know what you think about the purchase." Yes, it takes an extra moment, but your customers won't forget it.

Any little bonus you can include in your packaging to remind your customer about you is a plus, such as a business card, refrigerator magnet, or product samples and little freebies.

SELLER PROFILE: Zou Zou's Basement

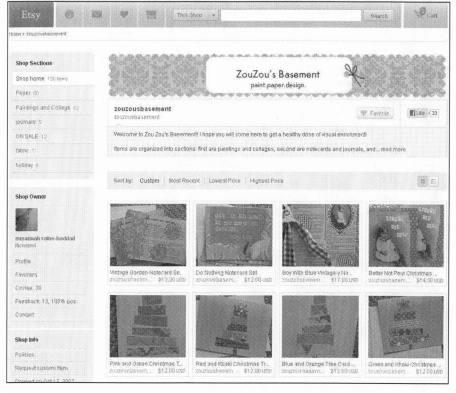

From her home studio in Richmond, Va., Susannah Raine-Haddad spends half her time painting, and the other half playing with paper to make unusual note cards. She's been in business for 20 years, but is planning to ramp up her sales using Etsy. See Etsy.com/shop/zouzousbasement.

How did you get started?

I've been painting, drawing and making cards since I was a child. I was an art major in college. One day I was helping my mother clean out my grand-mother's house, and we discovered about 100 terra cotta flower pots in her basement. I took some, painted them, and gave them as gifts. Then several people asked where they could buy one! So I started a business painting flower pots. That was about 20 years ago.

My business is named for my grandmother. She held on to all those terra cotta pots because she'd lived through the Great Depression.

How has your business changed?

Over the years, my media and subject matter have changed dramatically as I've changed as a person and grown as an artist. I started with flower pots, then began painting furniture and canvas floor mats. I began painting on glass. I went back to art school, and began more paintings and drawings.

I always had time constraints on my art. When my two children were born, I painted during their naptimes. I've taught art full time, but still wanted to concentrate on my own work.

Now I can paint every day for three hours. The business side also takes up a lot of time—an hour or so during the day, and few hours at night.

What inspires your projects?

I paint what I know. For example, I have been doing a series on dessert foods—I had been photographing desserts cases for years. I bake and eat sweets every day.

I concentrate on a few subjects at a time, then move on. My first decision is color. I tear things out of magazines, or do quick sketches when I see a color combination or particular shade I like.

How do you attract customers and get repeat business?

Most of my business is still local and word of mouth. I also send out a newsletter. I do farmers markets in the summer, selling mostly note cards, and art shows in the fall. I apply for shows and donate for auctions all the time. I have postcards printed with my work to give away. I'm on Facebook, and have a website.

How big is the online portion of your business?

About 50 percent of my business is from shows and farmers markets, about 20 percent is from direct inquiries and commissions, and 10 percent is online.

Two Crowned Cranes

ρ zoom

This 9" x 12" collage is made of painstakingly small cuts of paper to resemble the feathers
on these two cranes. The base is acrylic on gessoboard, sides are painted, ready to hang.
The hand cut patterned papers are in a variety of blacks, whites, reds, yellows, creams, and
greys. Based on a photo of real cranes with these headdresses!

More and more people are shopping online, so I'm on Etsy. My work gets a
lot of traffic, but it's a big challenge to sell expensive artwork online. More
inexpensive items, like cards, are easier to sell.

For years I just put my stuff in my shop and waited for people to come. Now I am working much harder at selling.

How do you price your items?

For note cards, I account for my costs of all materials, and also consider what "boutique" cards sell for, and price mine accordingly. For paintings, I also consider my cost of materials, and factor in the time spent painting. I don't really have an hourly rate. I price reasonably, but at a level to match what I have put into it. And I'll look at similar pieces out there, and price mine accordingly.

ETSY MARKETING ON A NICKEL (OR LESS)

Part of the beauty of Etsy is its vibrant community. Even if you're a rank beginner, membership gives you access to millions of paying customers and helpful advisers. So even if you're just starting your business, you're not starting from scratch, you're standing on a lot of shoulders.

Simply by paying the small listing fee of 20 cents per item, you get nice exposure on the Etsy marketplace. That's a great start, but there are many more techniques for maximizing your exposure and sales. Some people call these techniques "social media" marketing. Whatever you call it, they're good tools for getting shoppers to notice and buy your stuff.

Plug your items on Facebook and Twitter

Facebook and Twitter, two popular Web social networks, can help you find new customers and remind your old customers to return. It's a great way to promote your shop—not only is it free, but your customers will gladly do much of the work for you! Here's how to get started:

1. On Etsy, visit Shop Settings > Info & Appearances.

2. Midway down the page, you see a section labeled Links and a checkbox for Facebook and Twitter.

3. For Facebook, click the link Connect with Facebook. Then you'll see a log-in box, where you can enter your Facebook user name and password.

4. For Twitter, click the link Connect with Twitter and log into your account.

After you authorize the connection with Facebook:

• Shoppers will see a Like button for your Facebook Page below the banner of your Etsy shop.

• You'll be able to post items to your Facebook Page when you add them to your Etsy shop.

- Anyone who has Liked you on Etsy will see your Facebook Page updates in their Facebook News Feed.

After connecting your shop with Twitter:

- Shoppers will see a Follow button for your Twitter account below the banner of your Etsy shop.

- You'll be able to tweet about each new listing you add to your shop.

- Anyone who has "followed" you through Etsy will see your updates in their Twitter timeline.

| Info & Appearance | Sections | Policies | Shop Name | Languages |

Info & Appearance

Shop Banner Image [   ] [Browse...]

Upload a .jpg, .gif or .png that is 760px by 100px and no larger than 2MB. Get ideas.

Links ☐ Facebook Page   Link a Facebook Page with your shop

☐ Twitter Account   [🐦 Connect with Twitter]

Enable to gain Facebook fans and Twitter followers for your shop. Learn more.

Shop Announcement
English [   ]

This illustration shows the **Shop Settings>Info & Appearances** page in my Etsy account. At this point, I've clicked the blue **Connect with Facebook** button to log into my personal Facebook profile and authorize the connection with Etsy. The next step: registering at Facebook for a free "Facebook Page" for my business or shop name (see **Facebook.com/pages/create.php**) while logged into my personal Facebook Profile. Finally, I'll click the checkbox above for **Link a Facebook Page with your shop**. To view a video tutorial of this procedure, see **Etsy.com/connect**.

The Facebook "Page" for the Etsy shop Inedible Jewelry. Directly from Etsy, the page attracts friends who click the "Like" buttons on the shop's items, then receive tidbits of news about the shop and its offerings. These business-oriented Facebook pages, also known as "fan" pages, are separate from regular Facebook accounts for individuals.

After you've connected your Etsy account with Facebook, you'll see Facebook "Like" buttons on Etsy listing pages, shop pages, and Treasury lists. When Facebook members click the link, a link to the Etsy page and a thumbnail image of the page are posted on that member's Facebook profile. Members can add an optional comment to the post. Numerals next to the like button indicates how many Facebook members have "liked" the page.

Promote your shop on Facebook

If you want to get the most mileage out of Facebook, be sure to open an account in your business name, in addition to the personal Facebook Profile you may already have for connecting with friends and family. A business Facebook "Page," also known as a "fan" page, offers many more promotional features.

Another important detail: when you open the Facebook Page account for your business name, do so while you're logged into your personal Facebook Profile. This enables your Facebook Page to be "associated" with your Facebook Profile, and allows the "My Etsy" functions to function. Assuming you already have a personal Facebook Profile, then you're ready to open the Facebook Page for your shop name at Facebook.com/pages/create.php.

My Etsy application. After you've set up your Facebook Page, you can install the "My Etsy" application on your Page. (You can't use the app on your personal Facebook profile.)

Two key advantages of having a Page with "My Etsy" installed:

> ### Getting squared away with Facebook
>
> When you open your Facebook Page for your Shop name, do so **while you're logged into** your personal Facebook Profile. Why? Your personal Facebook Profile and your Facebook Page must be associated in order for the "My Etsy" functions to operate on your Page. If you already have a personal Facebook Profile, then you're ready to open the Facebook Page for your shop name at Facebook.com/pages/create.php.

- Visitors of your business Page can become "fans" and immediately get more information about your shop.

- Business pages allow you to post photos, videos, applications, discussion boards, wall postings, groups, and other interactive tools.

Tweet your horn on Twitter

Like Facebook, Twitter lets you promote yourself and your items to millions of online readers. But there's much more to Twitter; you can use it as a valuable market intelligence tool.

Sometimes it helps to see a visual tutorial on this topic. Etsy's support staff has a video tutorial explaining why and how to connect your shop with Twitter: Etsy.com/connect.

Connecting your Etsy account with Twitter enables you and your customers to easily share links to your shop and item listings. "Tweet" links on Etsy pages enable users with accounts at Twitter.com to easily share the link to the page with their Twitter followers. Twitter followers see the link as an "etsy.me" URL.

Use Etsy's URL shortener. If you want to share the URL of an Etsy page, the site has a built-in URL shortener. It creates an abbreviated version of the link, which requires less space in a Twitter "tweet" or Facebook status update.

To use the URL shortener, copy the URL from your Web browser's address bar and paste it into the blank at this Web page: bit.ly.

This creates a shorter, "etsy.me" version of the link. You don't need to have an account at bit.ly to use the service.

Offer a newsletter or blog based on your feed

Let's face it, a lot of people aren't on Facebook or Twitter. To reach these folks, you can offer a subscription service based on your Shop feed. Then people on your email list will receive news when you add new listings. (A word to the wise: Don't use Etsy's Convo feature to send your newsletters, as this is specifically prohibited by Etsy's Terms of Use.)

Why would you offer an email newsletter? Plenty of reasons:

- **Free advertising is the best advertising.** You have no better source of potential sales than your previous customers. A newsletter reminding them about your new listings can pay off more than a paid advertising campaign. It takes much more time, energy and money to attract a new customer compared with getting another sale from an old customer.

- **Build your brand.** When you keep your name in front of your customers, they're more likely to remember it while shopping, and to mention it to friends. Last year's customers might forget about you—unless you jog their memory with a newsletter.

- **Rise above the noise.** Not everyone pays attention to Facebook, Twitter, blogs, and feed readers. Even if they do, they don't always have time to keep up with it all. It's called information overload. An email with your shop name on it can cut through all that clutter. It gives you what marketing gurus call a "touchpoint" that can have a more immediate, personal feel than other social networks. Most everyone checks their email every day, while other things might slide.

Several third-party email subscription services let you send updates about your Etsy feed. These services also assist you in designing your newsletter, sharing them automatically on social networks like Facebook, and tracking results—such as who opens your messages, and which headlines or offers get the most interest. Then you can segment your list and send targeted offers to certain customer groups.

Among the most popular services:

- **MyEmma.com.** Costs about $30 to send your newsletter to 1,000 or fewer subscribers. The fee rises as your subscriber count goes up.

- **MailChimp.com.** Free for up to 2,000 subscribers. A paid service with a few extra features starts at $10 a month for up to 500 subscribers.

- **Aweber.com.** This full-featured service starts at $19 a month for up to 500 subscribers.

- **FeedBurner.com.** This service operated by Google includes a free email service, but is a bit more complicated to use and not as flexible as competing paid services.

Blogs. A blog is an easy way to offer an online newsletter that can also serve as a Web site. Get a free account at Blogspot.com.

Create coupon codes

Everyone likes a deal. Providing an extra incentive, such as a coupon, can be just the thing to persuade a shopper to buy. Once your Etsy shop is open for business, you can start creating custom coupon codes to offer special discounts in your shop. Shoppers are more likely to buy something—or something extra—when they believe they're getting a special offer. Coupon codes you create are redeemable only at your store, until you deactivate them.

You can create two types of Etsy coupon codes:

Percent Discount. Shopper gets a flat percentage deducted from their whole order from your shop. Shipping fees aren't included in calculating the discount. Sales tax, if any, is calculated on the discounted merchandise total, not the original price. Fifteen percent is a good place to begin experimenting. Percentage discounts are redeemable for anything in your store; you can't limit it to certain items or sections. Likewise, upon a sale you'll pay Etsy's 3.5-percent commission on the discounted total, not the original listed prices.

Free Shipping. Shipping fees are deducted from the buyer's order from your shop. You can restrict this offer to orders shipped within your home country.

To create a coupon code:

1. Visit Your Account > Coupon Codes, which appears in the sidebar under Promote.

2. Click the button for Create New Coupon.

3. To specify the code, enter at least five characters, but no more than 20, consisting of letters or numbers. Each code must be unique. To prevent confusion among customers, sellers aren't allowed to change code names or percentages after they activate the code.

4. Specify the coupon type from the dropdown menu—Percent Discount or Free Shipping.

5. Set the status, active or inactive. Click Add Coupon.

Deactivate coupon codes. To change the status of a coupon code, visit Your Account > Coupon Codes. Select a code, and you'll be prompted to activate or deactivate the code. Or you can delete a code by clicking the X on the right. After a code has been deactivated, shoppers won't be able to use it at checkout. After a code has been deleted, you can not resurrect it to use again in your shop.

Publicize your coupon code

Nobody will take advantage of your special deal unless they know it exists. So the more you publicize your coupon, the more sales it will help generate. Here are some good strategies for creating and publicizing your coupon code:

- **For every purchase.** Satisfied customers often return to buy again— especially when they receive an invitation to do so. Repeat customers are the lifeblood of any business. So keep them coming back with a discount code enclosed in your packages.

- **Share with friends.** Create a code for your Facebook friends and fans, pen pals, and Twitter followers. If you've got a blog or website, post a coupon code there. Encourage your friends and associates to pass the code onto their own networks.

- **For online links.** Do you have friends or associates who publish a blog? Create a discount code just for that audience, and track the results.

- **Link to advertising.** If you're paying to appear in any advertising—in local newspapers, for example, create a special code so you can track your results. (If you create a special code mentioned only in your advertising, you'll be able to measure the payoff from your ad dollars.)

- **For your team.** Got an Etsy team? Have everyone set up the same coupon code, and cross-promote them in your item listings.

- **For wholesalers.** Do you work with wholesalers? Create a coupon code just for them.

- **For everyone.** Offer something for everyone. Put a discount code in your shop announcement, banner, and profile.

Get your items on Google Product Search

If you're familiar with the Web, you know about Google, the world's most popular search tool. You can find all sorts of things merely by entering the right keywords at Google.com. Indeed, millions of people use Google to find things to buy. For example, if you search for "handmade wool scarf" on Google, the top result is an Etsy shop, That Funky Boutique, at Etsy.com/shop/ThatFunkyBoutique. You can bet that a lot of the shop's sales come from folks searching on Google who hadn't even heard of Etsy—or That Funky Boutique.

One of Google's most valuable innovations is the "shopping" results, where it displays products deemed to be of interest to Google users.

Fortunately, you don't have to pay anything, or be a technical whiz, to get this free exposure on Google. For the organic search results, Google indexes pages in your shop, recording the text and images. For Google Product Search, Etsy automatically submits a "feed" of your shop listings. As a result, your items will appear in Google search results when users search for relevant terms. Your listings will appear on Google with your shop name and feedback average. This exposure can prompt sales from Google users who weren't necessarily shopping at the moment, and weren't familiar with Etsy.

Just like local people-generated word of mouth, it takes a while to earn this free exposure with Google Product Search. If your shop is brand-new, it may take several weeks before Etsy includes your shop in the batch of listings it uploads to Google—known in Web parlance as a "syndication feed." Etsy doesn't include new sellers in the Google Product Search feed until they've recorded at least six sales and have some positive customer feedback. At least, that's Etsy's official policy; some sellers have been told by Etsy's support staff that it can take up to a year to get added to Etsy's Google feed.

Other sellers note that their traffic increased substantially, immediately after reaching 100 sales. Again, it's not an Etsy policy, but too big a coincidence to ignore.

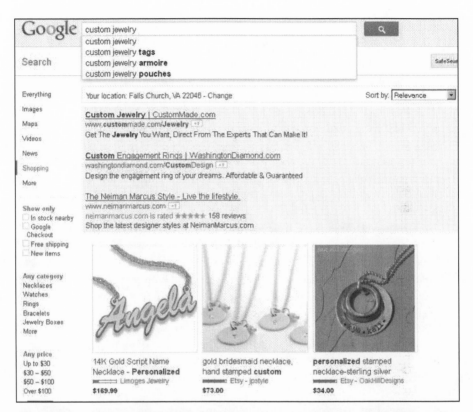

Lots of Etsy traffic originates with Google. Here, a Google "shopping" search shows listings for two Etsy stores in the bottom right corner. The top three links are paid advertisements appearing through Google's ubiquitous Adwords program. But for the moment, we're concentrating on the free, "organic" traffic that Google generates based on keywords in our shop listings.

Once you show up in the Google results, any changes you make in your Etsy shop, such as new listings or changes in your feedback score, take one or two days to show up.

Tweaking your listings for Google

Although Google and Etsy take care of most of the technical details, there are a few tricks that will ensure you get the best exposure. Google's Product Search program has some formatting and policy standards explained below. You can maximize your exposure here by ensuring your item listings agree with Google's policies—which sometimes conflict with standard practices at Etsy.

- **Long titles.** Listing titles on Etsy may use up to 140 characters, which can be valuable space for you to add descriptive keywords, refer to a special offer, or simply add special characters such as asterisks as an eye-catching device. But on Google Product Search, titles longer than 70 characters are truncated. If your item listings violate any of the Google Product Search policies listed below, they're automatically kicked out of Google's "shopping" results.

- **"Mature" content.** Item listings with mature content, as defined in Etsy's policies, aren't included in Etsy's feed to Google Product Search. So you'll need to depend on your customer finding your item directly through your shop, or by searching on Etsy. You simply won't get any shopping traffic for items tagged "mature" through Google.

- **Special characters like stars or hearts**. Listing titles or descriptions with these non-standard characters are filtered out by Google because they simply look weird on some computer displays. So, if you're creating a "bulleted" list of paragraphs in your listing description, use hyphens or asterisks at the start of each paragraph. Those fancy characters aren't really worth getting kicked off Google, are they?

- **Using boilerplate or promotional text.** If you include phrases like "free shipping" in your description, you won't show up in Google. You can confine such details to your Shipping Profiles and Shop Policies page.

- **Repeated, unneeded punctuation, capitalization, or symbols.** This is common practice on Etsy, but gets you kicked out of Google.

- **Duplicate listings.** After reading all the persnickety rules above, you might be tempted to simply create duplicate listings for all your Etsy items—one set of listings that conform to Google's rules, and another set of listings optimized for Etsy. In theory, duplicate listings would be a perfect way to fully expose your items to Etsy and Google users. Unfortunately, duplicate listings are weeded out by Google—otherwise, Google would be swamped with cookie-cutter listings. Furthermore, each Etsy listing requires an individual item you have on hand, ready to ship. Unless you have a stock of identical items on hand, there's a risk that duplicate listings would be bought simultaneously, and you'd have to cancel one of the sales—and make one of your customers very unhappy.

Deal directly with Google. As mentioned previously, Etsy handles the technical details of analyzing your shop listings and uploading a feed to Google Product Search. But someday you might also have a website of your own to generate sales directly to customers—or perhaps you already do. In that case, you'll want to generate a feed and upload it yourself to Google Product Search.

To get started, you'll open a free account with Google Merchant Center and register your feed. Then you'll create a file containing your item listings in a text file and upload it to Google by following the instructions provided with your merchant account.

To get started, visit Google.com/support/merchants.

SELLER PROFILE: Metalicious

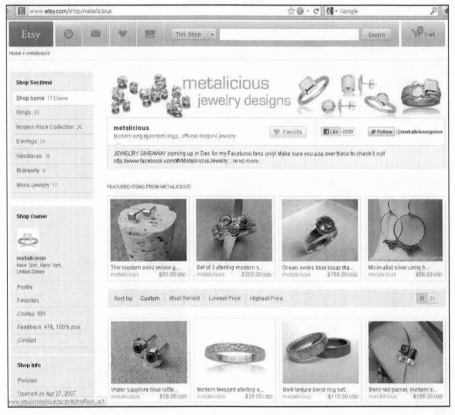

Stephanie Maslow is an active Etsy buyer and seller who makes and sells handmade, urban-inspired jewelry. A New York resident, she enjoys supporting other crafters, and even bought her coffee table through Etsy. See **Etsy.com/shop/metalicious**.

How did you get started?

Sixteen years ago I was in a boring job and was desperate for some creative challenges where I could use my hands. I went to the local art school, but the pottery class I was interested in was closed. Hmm—the only class with an opening was metal smithing.

On my jewelry bench, I still have what looks like a tin can I forged from copper. It reminds me how close I came to missing out on my true calling as a jeweler. I hammered my heart out, and have never looked back

How has your business evolved and how have you weathered tough times?

My business started as a part-time hobby to keep me in the jewelry business while I was raising my kids. It gave me something to do and a little extra cash. Once I decided to do it full time, I focused on gaining customers, both on Etsy and by growing my wholesale business.

You get such great exposure on Etsy to all kinds of people. I've had a few stores contact me because they saw my work there. I excel at customer service and special requests, so my shop and reputation grew from there.

What's your creative process?

I think three-dimensionally. I'm a nerd, and I love to build tiny things. Put that all together and you get my fun, cheeky line of jewelry.

I'm so busy with running my business and taking care of my kids that I don't have time to be still, so most of my ideas come to me in my down time—sleep. I'll wake up in the middle of the night with a "great" idea and jot it down on a sketch pad next to my bed. In the morning, if I still think it's a great idea, I'll go for it!

My past work as a merchant for department stores taught me a lot about expanding on successes and letting go of failures. It's still hard for me to admit when something isn't working, but when I put it in the perspective of what will earn me money to put food on the table, my ego always takes second place.

How do you find customers and get repeat business?

I work lots of angles. The first is advertising. Like most niche businesses, I don't have a lot of extra cash lying around, so I have to be really smart about where I spend it. I do lots of research online to find out where my customer is going, what they are reading, how they like to buy. Then I'll target those places—blogs, websites, etc.—and focus on getting my customer to come to my shop. I use Google Analytics to see how much traffic is being driven to my shop and where it's coming from.

14k pink rose gold ring set 2mm and 4mm wide shiny or satin finish

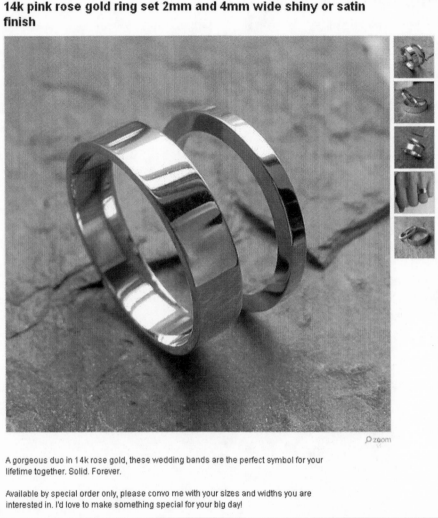

🔎 zoom

A gorgeous duo in 14k rose gold, these wedding bands are the perfect symbol for your lifetime together. Solid. Forever.

Available by special order only, please convo me with your sizes and widths you are interested in. I'd love to make something special for your big day!

The second angle is analyzing my target market: Why do people come to my shop, and what are they looking for?

Thirdly, it's refining my keywords. Search Engine Optimization is big on Etsy. They've worked really hard to figure out an algorithm to get the "right" customer into my shop. As long as I'm tagging my work with keywords my customer searches for, they will find me on Etsy and want to buy what I'm selling.

What share of your business is online versus shows and stores?

Eighty percent of my business is online, and 20 percent is whole-sale/consignment. The trend is that people have less time to shop in traditional stores. With their spare time, most people want to do hobbies, sports, and activities with their family or partners—not shopping. So I've seen a huge increase in my online sales over the past five years.

With smarter search engines, it's much easier for shoppers to find exactly what they're looking for online. So it's the perfect place for a savvy craftsperson to be now.

How do you price your items?

My cost of goods, plus the cost of my time, equals the cost of my item. I multiply that by 1.6 to get my selling price.

I make everything painstakingly by hand, and my customers appreciate that. If they want cheap, they know to go somewhere else. My prices reflect my time and what it takes to support my family. People appreciate knowing where their jewelry is coming from, and supporting American craftspeople—and I'm so thankful that they do!

FIND AND SELL VINTAGE ITEMS

Etsy recognized something that artisans have always known: artists and art-lovers often also appreciate antiques and vintage wares. And, frankly, some of us are better at recognizing a great item than we are at creating them. So Etsy permits the sale of vintage items made more than 20 years ago. If you're regularly spotting interesting knickknacks at garage sales and other places, you'll find a robust market for them on Etsy—as long as you price and describe them creatively and appropriately.

The vintage category is one of the fastest-growing on Etsy, and loaded with opportunity. If you're a savvy trader, you can turn up dozens, perhaps hundreds of resellable gems each week. You'd be hard-pressed to hand-craft that many items!

Often you'll need to research an item to discover how rare, old, or desirable it is. One popular reference is *Antique Trader Antiques & Collectibles 2012 Price Guide,* which is available at many libraries. Another way to research pricing is to search completed transactions at eBay for the same item.

A related area gaining traction on Etsy is recycling items or materials for a new use, sometimes called "upcycling." For example, a crafter might fashion a hat from old napkins, or saw the bottoms off used wine bottles for reuse as jars or drinking glasses.

Having a separate shop for vintage

One of the dangers in selling vintage items is the potential for confusion among Etsy buyers. Some of them aren't aware that vintage items are sold on the site. Every once in a while, an unwitting Etsy shopper will buy a vintage item and become outraged to find that's it's a used item, not a new, hand-crafted item.

To avoid such confusion, some Etsy sellers have an entirely separate shop and user name for their vintage items. At a minimum, you should have separate shop sections for any vintage stock, and give appropriate disclosures in your item descriptions.

Artist Jill Morrison of Lawrence, Kansas, crafted this unique living-room couch from a discarded cast-iron claw foot bathtub. As she originally found it, the tub might have made an excellent "vintage" item on Etsy, but she upcycled for a different, eye-catching use. It won first place in a design competition of recycled Etsy items sponsored by NBC Universal.

See Morrison's shop, Ruff House Art, at **Etsy.com/shop/ruffhouseart**.

Developing a vintage niche

Are you an expert on vintage board games? Antique clocks? Old radios? Consider making this your Etsy vintage specialty. The more you deal with a certain type of item, the better you'll learn how to find it at a bargain and resell it profitably.

You can start gathering merchandise from your own attic, basement, or closet. Thrift stores, rummage sales, and even unwanted gifts can produce valuable finds:

- Old radios, stereos and electronic equipment. Don't assume that old cassette or 8-track tape player is worthless. You might be surprised how much some of your old "junk" is worth.

- Old sports equipment such as fishing rods, baseball bats, basketballs, exercise devices, and uniforms.

- Unused wedding, anniversary, and birthday gifts. Turn that deadwood into cash and build your track record on Etsy.

- Old books, videos, and games you don't plan to use anymore. Out-of-print items are particularly valuable.

- Old clothes, bathing suits, and shoes. Everything comes back into style sooner or later, and "vintage" clothing has never been hotter.

You can find gems just about anywhere, including thrift shops and charity marts run by Goodwill, the Salvation Army, etc. Can you make good money by marking up the items you find at these shops and reselling them on Etsy? Sure, and the stores are grateful for each dollar you spend there, which helps fund their programs. But remember a few caveats. When buying vintage or antique small appliances, housewares, toys, furniture, and other items, remember to abide by Etsy's rule prohibiting the sale of recalled items. For example, did you know that most Corningware coffee percolators have been recalled? Also, you probably shouldn't resell an antique crib on Etsy unless you stated in your listing, "This item is sold for decorative use only and not intended as a place for a child to sleep."

Develop sources of vintage items

To find items that can be resold profitably, you'll need to find sources in your area where used items are actively traded at bargain prices. After a while, you'll discover which places are best, and make those parts of your regular rounds. Here's where to start:

Estate sales. Estate sales can be wonderful sources of vintage items and valuable antiques. These sales liquidate the entire contents of a household and can include large collections of rare items. They are often advertised in newspaper ads, but you can also subscribe to email alerts for estate sales at Estatesales.net.

If you attend an estate sale, plan on being the first in the door. This can mean standing in line for 45 minutes or more at a well-publicized sale, but getting first crack at the goodies can be worth the wait. Bring cash or your checkbook, as many estate sales operate like garage or yard sales—no credit card machines.

Most estate sales are held on Friday or Saturday mornings. Larger sales may begin on Thursday and continue through Sunday. Remaining items are usually marked down 50 percent on the last day, so a good sale may be worth a second visit. But don't pass up good finds on Friday or Saturday because you think you'll get them more cheaply on Sunday. By then, 98 percent of the cream will be skimmed. Get the good stuff while you can.

If there are more estate sales advertised on a given Saturday than you have time to attend, it's worth doing some detective work to determine which sales are likely to have the best quantity and selection of items. Sales on Estatesales.net typically include photos; the newspaper ad should have a contact number for the liquidator running the sale. Phone ahead and ask for details on what's for sale.

If estate sales work well for you, it's worthwhile to cultivate a relationship with the estate liquidators who work the sales in your area. Leave your business card and ask to be notified of all sales.

Auctions. Like estate sales, auctions can be a gold mine of vintage items. Auctions are typically held on the weekend, beginning on Fridays, and usually advertised in newspapers. If you're fortunate enough to live near an auction house, phone ahead for their schedule, as some sales occur on weeknights.

Auction buying has a learning curve. It's best to attend your first one with an experienced buyer if possible, or arrive a bit early so you can obtain instructions from the staff. Auction houses often ask buyers to register upon arrival, so be prepared to show your drivers' license. You'll be assigned a number on a card or paddle which you'll display when bidding on items. When you're ready to leave, you'll turn in your number and the staff will have a list of your winning bids. After paying your bill, you'll carry out your purchases.

Auction houses rarely charge for admission, but there's usually a "buyers premium," an additional amount you'll owe in addition to your winning bids.

Premiums range from about 2 percent to 12 percent. Credit cards are usually accepted at auctions, and often a modest discount is offered for payments in cash or check.

Auctions featuring antiques and collectibles are usually worthwhile for Etsy sellers. At the start, premium items are usually auctioned, followed by box lots of perhaps less-desirable items. Bargain-priced lots often contain one or two hidden gems for sellers, even if most of the lot turns out to be junk. Because all items are available for viewing before the sale, you can decide what's worth bidding on beforehand. At most sales, you're allowed to touch, poke, and handle items before they are up for auction.

Thrift shops. Thrift shops can be worthwhile for vintage scouting if the store gets new stock in often enough. Unfortunately, some charity thrifts like Goodwill stores have begun selling their best items online, so the stock may have been cherry-picked already. Fortunately, the picking is usually done by part-time volunteers, not eagle-eyed sellers, so bargains often remain.

Church thrift shops are a potential source of stock too, however. The prices are usually reasonable and the donated items are often of higher quality than those at commercial thrift shops.

Classified ads. If you have trouble finding enough stock using the sources discussed above, try a classified advertisement.

If you place an ad offering to pay people cash, you'd better be ready for a response. The challenge is keeping the nuisance responses to a minimum. Don't give anyone the impression that you're itching to spend a wad of cash on any junk. Keep expectations low. One strategy that seems to work is offering a "finder's fee" for referrals to a collection you agree to buy.

Ads in metropolitan daily newspapers are costly, so look for alternatives such as weekly newspapers and circulars like *Penny Saver* and *Thrifty Nickel*.

Craigslist. Craigslist.com, a free online classified ads site, is a great place to look for vintage items that you can resell. Sometimes, the inventory is available free—browse the "free" section under the "For Sale" category. A lot of these items are leftovers from garage sales, or stuff being cleared out by people who couldn't be bothered to have a garage sale.

If you're an iPhone user, check out the CraigsPro app. It has a nice interface for browsing ads and posting to Craigslist. Also, the app lets you run automatic searches of Craigslist for certain items, and sends you the results via "push" notifications. You can search multiple cities, view a map browser, search results with photos, and more. For more information, search your phone's app store for "Craigslist."

Two similar apps are available for Android phones: "Craigslist" and "Craigslist Browser."

Freecycle. Freecycle.org is another Internet outlet for free stuff. Often, you'll simply notice that someone has placed such-and-such at the curb, and the first person who sees it gets to have it. But don't advertise the fact that you might resell the items. Some people on Freecycle are quite high-and-mighty about the site being "nonprofit" and get prickly if they sense someone might earn a buck rescuing an item from a landfill, which is the whole point of Freecycle. But, you know, some people can't see the forest for the trees.

Garage sales and yard sales. Weekend neighborhood sales can be a decent source of stock if you enjoy wheeling and dealing. Garage and yard sales require lots of legwork, though, and the proportion of junk to gems is high.

The main problem is that these sales are full of the stuff people no longer want, which contrasts with an estate sale that liquidates the entire contents of a household. Some yard salers have caught on to this difference and now advertise their garage sales as "estate sales," aiming to draw more buyers. When you're scanning the classifieds, beware of yard sales masquerading as estate sales. An "estate sale" that does not advertise items like furniture, silver, and stemware might be a yard sale in disguise.

Items on consignment. If enough people know you're a dealer of vintage items, eventually someone may ask you to sell some of their stuff. Presumably, you'd earn a commission on sales, and this option can be a tempting way to acquire inventory, but it carries pitfalls and can be a distraction. To do it right, you'd need to set up a bookkeeping system for consignments. You would also need good insurance coverage if you had stock on hand that you didn't own in the event of fire, flood, or some other disaster.

If items offered for consignment look good to you, offer to buy them outright. Sell them yourself and avoid the hassles of a consignment deal. Television shows such as "Antiques Roadshow" have convinced too many people that treasures are lurking in their attic or basement. Most of the stuff isn't valuable, it's just old. You don't want to be roped into storing someone's worthless junk.

Library sales. For vintage books, it's hard to beat a library sale. Sales are often conducted monthly, usually on a Saturday, and feature a wide variety of books at very low prices. Nearly all the books are priced at a dollar or two apiece, and plenty can be resold for $10 or more online.

Most library sales are organized by a nonprofit Friends of the Library (FOL) group, and most of the books for sale are donated by area residents in very good or like-new condition. Because the library can't absorb most of this material into its collection, the surplus is offered for public sale as a fund-raiser. So, you'll find plenty of books at library sales with no library markings whatsoever. Plus, the right book, even if it has library markings, can be worth a pretty penny.

The nice thing about selling books is that you'll occasionally stumble onto a really valuable collectible book worth $50 or more, just in the course of your regular buying. So it's smart to check the value of a book by typing the title and author name into Amazon.com. Be sure to check for the price of the edition you have, not a current paperback copy, which is usually much cheaper.

Some book sales are better than others. Where there are large populations, there are lots of books, and sales near bigger cities tend to have more potential inventory. Books are also plentiful in college towns, and lots of them get donated to college-town libraries. Transient populations near universities and military bases leave lots of their books behind when they move on, too.

If you can't find good library sales in your area, try looking a bit farther afield—it may be worth the drive. Look in the newspaper classifieds and consult the website www.BookSaleFinder.com. Here, book sale dates are listed by city several months in advance, and you can subscribe to email alerts of upcoming sales. The site also has classified ads from used-book buyers and sellers. If you travel out of town for a book sale, combine the trip with visits to the area's used bookshops and thrift stores. You might find an overlooked bargain.

Vintage and handmade. Another possible specialty for Etsy sellers is selling upcycled vintage products. Not only is upcycling desirable from a "green" perspective—all vintage trade is a form of recycling—it can offer nostalgic value, memories of simpler times, and appreciation from those who recognize fine craftsmanship.

When you use a vintage item as the raw material for your handmade art, home décor, or houseware items, you have a foot firmly planted in all of Etsy's main markets. Some examples:

- Journals and cards made from collaged paper ephemera.

- Vintage hard suitcases repurposed into coffee tables.

- Broken antique china made into pendants.

Remember when you sell something you have upcycled or created using vintage items, you should categorize them on Etsy as "handmade," not vintage.

If your aesthetic is in the realm of tattered or "shabby chic," or if you love altered art and collage, you can sell your upcycled art not only in this niche, but as supplies for other like-minded artists as well.

SELLER PROFILE: Nestle and Soar

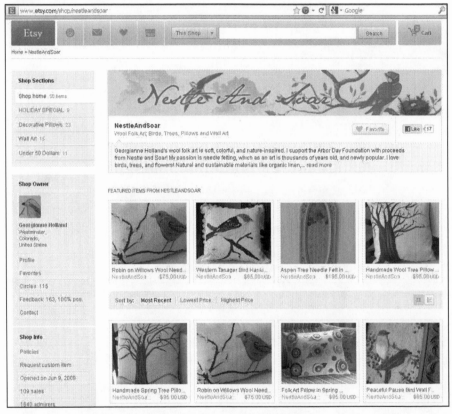

A folk art fiber artist, Georgianne Holland of Westminster, Colo., makes wool pillows and wall art featuring birds and trees. See Etsy.com/shop/nestleandsoar.

How did you begin?

I learned to love needle crafts when I was 11 years old. I sewed my own clothes on my mom's sewing machine, I taught myself embroidery, and loved all kinds of home-decor projects. I thought of myself as a little "Suzy Home-maker" and home arts became important to me at this young age.

My parents had founded and operated a successful family-owned quilting business, and this nurtured my love of folk art, too.

For the past six years I've focused on the ancient craft of needle felting. I use many of the same techniques used hundreds of years ago, taking an animal's

fluffy fleece and condensing it into durable, lovely items.

What brought you to Etsy?

I learned of Etsy on a television program— Joy Behar of "The View" mentioned that her daughter sold baskets on Etsy, which piqued my interest. I became a frequent customer of other Etsy artists because it was so fun and easy to shop there. At the time, I was designing my first line of bird-themed throw pillows, along with accessories like purses and jewelry.

The imagery of birds is my artistic focus, and also my kids were all going off to college or had already graduated, so I saw them soaring out into the world. I also saw myself as entering a new part of my life, the next stage, and that would involve a leap of faith, so I decided to claim that exciting time in my life!

How did you decide to focus your Etsy shop?

In the beginning, the product mix I placed in my Etsy shop was simply a little bit of everything I was making at the time, sort of like a garage-sale approach. After a few months, I realized that to be successful, I'd need to fine-tune the offerings using my theme. I removed everything from my shop that was not bird- or tree-related, and that's when my Etsy shop took off.

What skills do you bring into this?

I have been a needle arts teacher for 24 years, and I often host classes in my home studio. I design and publish patterns so that others can enjoy needle felting. I'm trying to keep up with technology like blogging and Facebook— I'm a low-tech girl in a high-fiber world. Fortunately, my kids all grew up with computers, so they often come to my rescue.

How has your business evolved and survived the tough economy?

Before Etsy, I was fortunate to have participated in a family-owned business, which was a big advantage. However, I had to learn the difference between operating a mail-order business and a real-time Internet boutique. Both business models depend on your ability to sell by using your written words. But Etsy is so much more immediate, it requires a different approach than the direct mail techniques that worked so well.

Western Tanager Bird Hankie Pillow, vintage, cushion, refurbished, needle felt, yellow bird

I have combined forces with a woman from 1940 to create this lovely designer pillow. This new series of hankie pillows are so much fun to create! I begin with a lovely, pristine vintage hankie, one that has lots of hand embroidery or tatting on the edge. I then choose a lovely bird specimen to hand needle felt onto the hankie; this is the Western Tanager...at least my interpretation of it! I have added a bit more embroidery and sewn it into a lovely nature-inspired pillow perfect as an accent in most every home.

12"x12" pillow with pillow insert included
Spot Clean pillow
Original design by Georgianne Holland, 2011.

Another lesson I learned on Etsy relates to the tough economy. The fiber folk art I make is a luxury item—no one *needs* fancy bird pillows. So when money is tight, many Etsy shoppers look, and don't purchase. That's one reason I'm developing patterns for my designs I'll sell in my shop. Some folks in this economy would rather learn how to make something instead of buying the finished piece. I love to pass along what I have taught myself. So I plan to continue making limited-edition items, original one-of-a-kind art, and will have a newsletter with opportunities to learn this craft using my design aesthetic.

How do you get repeat business?

My main tactic is providing smashing customer service. For instance, my handmade throw pillows are special, so to communicate that quality, I sew a pillow case to protect the pillow in transit to my customers. I wrap the reusable pillowcase closed with a silk or lace ribbon. It's like receiving a gift when you open the box!

How do you price your items?

I use what my dad called "fully loaded cost analysis." That includes not only your cost of goods, but your cost of selling. Many sellers on Etsy do not do this, and are willing to sell .their work for less than their total costs. Some don't even consider the time it takes to make the item.

However, there are many shopkeepers who are building their online boutique to earn a sustainable living, and that requires knowing and managing your true, or fully loaded, cost of sales.

It is a tricky environment for pricing when you are competing not only within, say, a geographic area of 10 square miles, but with shops all around the world. It's both challenging and fun.

MINE THE ETSY COMMUNITY

A great source of information and commentary about Etsy is the company's official blog, Etsy.com/blog. It's like a free online magazine, updated daily with articles, photos and videos about Etsy.

On the top navigation bar of Etsy's blog you'll see five sections:

- **Read.** Go directly to the most recent blog articles.

- **Watch**. See the most recent tutorials, seller profiles, and other videos.

- **Make.** Links to crafting how-to articles and videos.

- **Shop**. See the most recent "Featured Sellers" and other shopping articles

- **About us**. Etsy's mission statement, profiles of the blog's editorial staff, and instructions for pitching your own story idea for Etsy's blog.

You can stay abreast of the Etsy blog by following the links in the right sidebar under the Stay in Touch heading. The links allow you to get blog updates via Facebook, Twitter, and other avenues. If you use a feed reader like Google Reader to read online content, visit the list of Etsy blog feeds here: Etsy.com/blog/en/feeds.

Etsy forums

A gold mine of information is at your fingertips at Etsy's forums. These message boards function as a vehicle for seeking and dispensing advice, staying abreast of technical changes or snafus, or simply socializing. The most valuable thing about the forums is the immediate assistance you can obtain, free of charge, from other Etsy shop owners. It's like having a 24-hour consultant working for you, with no fees.

To reach the forums, visit Etsy.com, click Community at the top left of the page, then click Forums in the left sidebar. Among the most active forums are "Site Help" and "Business Topics." The official "Announcements" from Etsy's staff is must reading because many essential tidbits appear here that don't appear elsewhere, including email announcements.

The official Etsy blog, formerly known as "The Storque."

To get involved with an Etsy forum:

- Click a headline, or "thread" of interest. You'll see the original message, followed by replies.

- To respond, click Post a Reply at the top or bottom of the page.

- Type your post, and click Post a Reply. Your message will appear at the bottom of the thread.

You can view all threads where you've posted a reply by clicking Your Threads in the left sidebar, and then the tab Threads You've Posted In. If you want to monitor a thread that you haven't posted to, open the thread and click Mark. Then, to view these threads, go to the Your Threads page and click the Marked Threads tab.

Tapping the Etsy community

It's hard to overestimate the wealth of knowledge, technical solutions, business ideas, and suggestions you can reap, absolutely free, from Etsy's forums. Tapping that knowledge and wisdom can help you get your Etsy business off the ground, keep it on the right track, and out of the ditch. Etsy's administrative staff monitors the forums closely, so it's a good place to voice your opinion about Etsy features.

On the other hand, disagreements and heated discussions can create a distraction, and take away valuable time you could spend on your business.

Creating Treasury lists. This member-curated shopping gallery is made up of lists of four to 16 items. You can create an unlimited number of Treasuries to feature your favorite items, organized by theme, craft type, or other criteria. Etsy members can view your Treasury and post comments. You can see how many times your Treasury is viewed by other members by consulting the list's Stats section. Treasury isn't intended as a self-promotional tool for sellers, so don't select your own items.

To create a Treasury listing:

Click the Treasury link at Etsy's home page or Buy page, then click the Create a List link under Curator Tools.

- Treasury is designed for members to share favorite items on Etsy, and the lists, or part of a Treasury, are sometimes chosen by Etsy's staff for display on the home page.

- **Choose Listings.** Specify 16 items by providing the URL (web-page address) or listing ID for each item.

- **Title.** Think of an eye-catching name. Many are based on a seasonal theme, or a familiar catchphrase or quotation, such as, "Life is Like a Box of Chocolates," "Wouldn't It Be Nice," or "Autumn in the Country."

- **Description:** Explain how you thought of the list. This will appear below your finished Treasury list. Your profile thumbnail and user name appear here. Some simply say, "Enjoy!"

- **Privacy:** You can make the list private, accessible only to you, or public, visible to everyone.

- **Tags.** Think of keywords that apply to your list, which can help people find it via searches. Your tags should describe your group of items, not individual listings. For the tags you specify, your list will appear on the Treasury Web page for that tag, such as Etsy.com /treasury/tags/hats.

When you're ready to publish your Treasury, click the Save button at the bottom of the page. You can edit the list by clicking the Edit button on the right. You can add or delete items while you hover your cursor over the item image. Drag and drop the images to adjust their order in your list.

Moderate comments. As curator, you can delete comments from other members if you don't want them to appear with your list. Hover your mouse over the comment to see the Delete option.

Expose your list. Etsy's admin staff selects some Treasury items to be featured on the site's home page. To ensure your list is competitive, strive for variety. Don't include more than one item from a single shop, and don't include items from your own store.

Share your list. Treasuries have several features enabling you to easily share them with friends on social-networking sites like Facebook and Twitter. Click the Facebook or Twitter buttons in the right column to share your list.

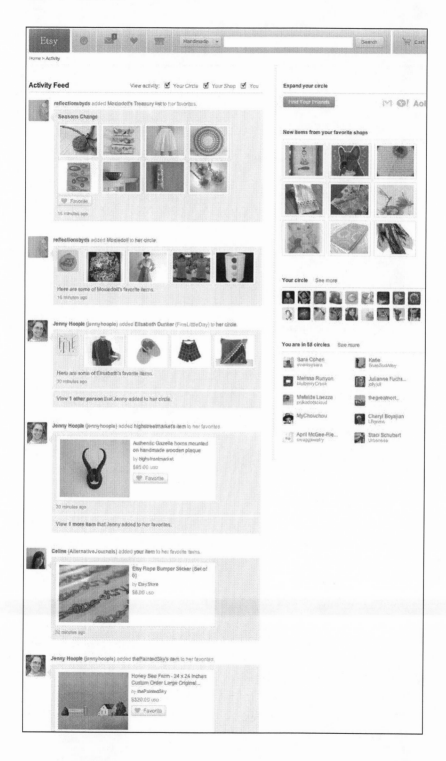

Deal with mature content. By default, Etsy filters Treasury lists with "mature" tags.

Members who create lists that might be objectionable to general audiences are asked to tag the Treasury "mature." As a result, when new members (or visitors who aren't signed into an Etsy account) click a link to a "mature" list, they receive a warning.

Etsy members who want to view Treasury lists without receiving warnings can adjust their account preferences. Visit Your Account > Settings > Preferences, and select Show me everything in Treasury, including mature content.

Members who are signed in who have selected Show me everything will be taken directly to the list.

Searching Treasury. You can search for Treasuries containing certain titles, tags and items using the search bar on any Treasury page. Ensure the dropdown menu in the search bar matches Treasury. You can also use search operators to refine your search, including:

- curator:

- shop:

- tags:

- title:

For example, to find all Treasury lists by the curator FineSilk, you would enter into the Treasury search bar:

curator:FineSilk

If you curate your own Treasury, a link to it will appear on your profile page under the heading Treasury Lists.

When, as a seller, one of your items appears in a Treasury, Etsy will add a link to that Treasury in that item's description. It's a nice boost when your items appear in a Treasury and it results in sales.

As a courtesy, curators will often notify you via Convo when they've included one of your items in a Treasury. Their message may urge you to visit and post a comment on the Treasury, and promote it on social networks like Facebook. The more page views and comments a Treasury receives, the more likely it will be selected to appear on Etsy's home page.

As a seller, you should check your Activity Feed regularly to see if you've been included in a Treasury.

Draw your Circles

Part of Etsy's value is not only in helping shoppers find unique and interesting things to buy, but to help its users connect with other crafters and other like-minded shoppers. Etsy's Circles feature is intended to do just that—help you keep track of friends and acquaintances who run Etsy shops, friends and family members who shop on the site.

When you first register, your Circle will be empty. As you add colleagues and shops to your Circle, you'll see content from them on your "activity feed" and you'll know when they list a new item or publish a Treasury.

To add members to your Circle, click the Add to Circle button on that person's profile page. View your circle by clicking the Circles link on the sidebar of your profile page. To see who's added you to their circles, click the Circles you're in tab on your activity feed. Also, you can search for Etsy members by user name or their real name, if it's part of their public profile—click the Search for members tab.

To view your Circle:

1. Visit your Etsy profile and click the Circles link on the left sidebar.

2. Click the Your Circle tab.

After you're registered at Etsy, "Find Your Friends" is another way to quickly locate acquaintances who are already members. The tab is in the Circle section of your profile. You can import your G-Mail, Yahoo or AOL Mail contacts. You'll see a list of those who are Etsy members, and you can click the Invite them link to send an invitation. The invitee receives an invitation showing your user name, avatar, shop listings and favorites. If they accept the invitation, they're added to your Circle, and you're added to theirs.

Etsy allows only 20 such invitations per day.

Deleting members from your circle. If you decide to remove a member from your circle, navigate to the person's profile page. In the sidebar, hover over the word "In," and a blue X will appear. Click the X to remove the member.

Etsy sends an email notifying members if you add them to your circle, but no message is sent if you remove them.

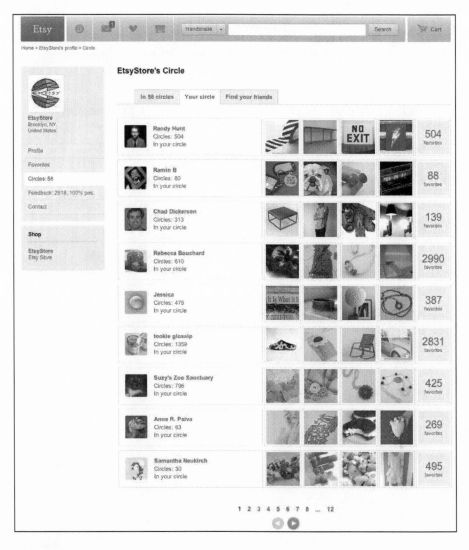

Activity feeds

Your "activity feed" is a Web page on Etsy that summarizes your activity on Etsy and the actions of people in your circle. By default it shows types of activity, such as adding items and shops to your Favorites list, creation of Treasury lists, and adding people to your Circle. You can view your activity feed here: Etsy.com/your/activity.

Privacy for Circles and Activity Feeds

By default, you share several things about your Etsy activity with other members, including favorites and purchase history, via Circles and Activity Feeds. If you wish, you can make several adjustments to keep certain things private.

Email notifications. When someone adds you to their Circle, Etsy sends you an email about it by default. If you'd rather not receive these emails, visit Your Account> Settings > Emails. You'll still have a way of discovering who's added you to your circle: Go to your public profile, click Circle, then click Circles you're in.

Purchase History. Etsy purchases are private, and when leaving feedback for sellers, your user name doesn't appear with it. (The seller, however, can see who left the feedback.) Likewise, feedback messages left by other members on your account aren't publicly visible; only your feedback average is shown. Your purchase history isn't visible to other members via activity feeds.

Favorites. In your account settings, if you've made your favorite items and shops "private" they won't appear in other members' activity feeds, regardless of whether you're in their Circle. If your settings are "public," then members who've added you to their Circle will be shown these items.

To adjust your privacy settings for favorites, visit Your Account > Settings > Privacy.

Blocking

By default, when someone adds you to their Circle, you're added automatically, and they can then view your information in their activity feed. If you don't want to be in someone's Circle or allow them to see your actions in their feed, you can block them. Visit their profile and click the Block link at the left bottom corner. Members won't receive a notification you've blocked them.

To unblock a member, visit their profile and click the Unblock link at the bottom left corner. After you've unblocked someone, they must add you to their Circle again to establish the connection.

Favorites and hearts

As mentioned previously, when you find an Etsy item or shop you'd like, you can bookmark it by adding it to your Favorites—it's also known as "hearting" an item or shop. Click the link that says Add to favorites in the right column of an item or shop page.

You can also mark favorites while viewing search results. Hover your cursor over a listing thumbnail, and a heart icon appears above the image. Click the heart to add the item to your favorites without having to visit the listing page.

To visit your Favorites list, click the heart icon in the gray header atop any Etsy page.

To browse favorites of other members, click the Favorites link on their profiles.

While viewing an item or shop, you can see who hearts it by clicking "See who hearts this" in the left column.

Click the various checkboxes at the top of your Activity Feed to filter your feed to show just items about your shop, you, or people in your circle. As mentioned previously, you can control what parts of your Activity Feed are visible to other members by adjusting your Favorites privacy setting.

Secret Admirers

Usually, anyone who views your Etsy profile can view the items or shops you've hearted. Likewise, if a shopper visits an Etsy shop or views a listing, they can view a list of Etsy members who've hearted that item or shop by clicking See Who Favorites This.

If you wish, you can keep your Favorites private. Here's how to be a "secret admirer" of a shop or listing, instead of being publicly identified:

1. Visit Your Account > Settings.

2. Click the Privacy tab.

3. Click Only You under Favorites.

4. Click the Update Privacy Settings button.

Etsy's 'Colors' shopping tool

In addition to Etsy's most popular shopping tools, searching and browsing, another way to discover items is the Colors tool, which tempts shoppers with items they might not have discovered otherwise.

Etsy's Colors feature presents a palate of colors and shades, and finds matching handmade items, vintage goods, and supplies based on your selection. To use the Colors tool, visit: Etsy.com/color.php

Gift ideas for Facebook friends

Etsy's tool "Gift Ideas for Facebook Friends" enables members to connect through the social-networking service based on your Etsy profile. Etsy suggests items to you based on the "likes" and "interests" of your Facebook friends. The Facebook feature has four main privacy safeguards:

1. Your personal Etsy data isn't shared through Facebook.

2. The tool won't post to your Facebook Wall unless you request it.

3. Etsy doesn't contact your Facebook friends.

4. You can "disconnect" the tool whenever you choose.

To use Gift Ideas, navigate to Etsy's "gift ideas" page from the Etsy home page, and click the Choose a Facebook Friend button. After you grant access to the Etsy tool through your Facebook account, you can browse or search your Facebook friends, highlight a name, and click OK. Etsy will suggest items based on your friend's Facebook profile. To explore further, click See more, or Choose Another Friend.

Gift Ideas can use only that information that your Facebook friends have designated as "public," so it doesn't function with Facebook members who keep their profiles "private," or haven't provided much information for their profile. Visit Etsy.com/gifts.

Here are some Etsy items that appear based on the "likes" of my Facebook friends. Pretty cool, huh?

People Search

People search helps you find Etsy members, even those with only a shopper's account. Use the drop-down menu from Etsy's search bar to refine your search to "People." You can search by user name, first name, or last name.

People search results are sortable, by relevance or alphabetically. From the displayed results, you can view profiles, preview their favorite items, and add the person to your Circle.

First and last names of Etsy members are searchable only if they've chosen to display their real name on their profile.

Etsy teams

Etsy Teams helps you meet and collaborate with people sharing common interests. Likewise, Etsy shoppers can find items and artisans they like through Etsy teams.

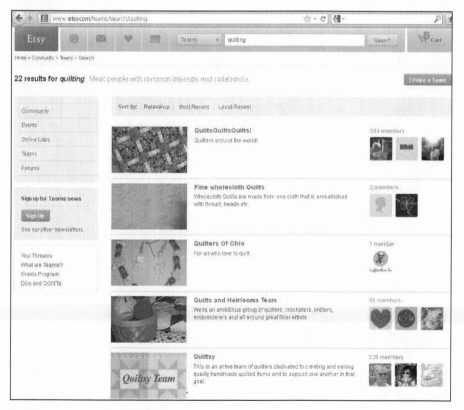

An Etsy team search for 'quilting.'

You can join an existing team, or start a new one. Each team has a captain who appoints one or more "leaders" who help run the ship.

To join a team, click the Join This Team button in the top left of the team page. Some teams are open to anyone, while others require certain qualifications you can review by clicking the Who can join? button on the team page. For example, here are the requirements for joining the Etsy Greek Street Team:

Apply to Team

Etsy Greek Street Team is a **moderated team**. Your application will be reviewed by a team leader.

Before you join Etsy Greek Street Team, please note the team charter:

- You need to have an active shop (items listed)
- If you are Greek or located in Greece and like to join us
use the application link "Apply to Group" provided in the sidebar

Greek team's tag: EGST
Add this tag to your listings

There are also 2 more steps you have to complete

1. Join to team's group on FLICKR
http://www.flickr.com/groups/etsygreekteam/

2. Join to team's YAHOO group
http://groups.yahoo.com/group/egst/
Please add your name and etsy shop name when you send a request to join the yahoo group
after you're been approved add your shop in database.

Joining to yahoo group is the best way to keep in touch with team's activities and receive mails and updates about them

Apply to Team   Cancel

To find a team you're interested in:

- Click the Community link at the top of an Etsy page.

- Click Teams on the left of the page.

- Enter a keyword in the search box and click Search. Etsy will show a list of teams matching your keyword.

Etsy's teams date back to the company's early days when sellers from a certain locale would form a "street team" to generate local word-of-mouth for their crafts. But thanks to the Internet, disparate crafters from around the globe who share a passion about, say, ragdolls, can unite as an Etsy team.

Teams originate with myriad themes and purposes:

- The "Made in Israel" team includes Etsian artists and designers who reside in Israel. The team exists to help one another share ideas and promote each other.

- "Soapers Haven" is intended for like-minded soap makers who want to exchange ideas, encourage each other, and enjoy each other's conversation.

- Often, an Etsy team will function similarly to an Etsy forum. The "Etsy Ideas" team functions much like a forum on business topics, but like other teams, is self-moderated. For example, the "Business Topics, Refined" team's charter is to explore business topics "without personal attacks, thread derailment, or snide remarks." Troublemakers are ejected "at first strike," the captain promises.

Teams are self-organizing and self-monitoring. Etsy takes no responsibility for the membership practices or any other team activities.

Anyone who's at least 18 years old can start an Etsy team. Forming a team automatically makes you its captain. A team has only one captain, but can have several "leaders" who are selected by the captain to assist with various responsibilities. Depending on the size of the team, leaders might help with:

- Evaluating applications of new members

- Inviting members

- Moderating the team's discussion forum

- Removing members

Starting your own team

To create a team, go to the Teams page, Etsy.com/teams, and click the **Create a Team** button. Describe your initial concepts for the team. You can embellish things later:

- **Name.** Choose a nickname with a catchy, meaningful few words. Search the existing teams to ensure someone isn't already using the same name or a nearly identical one.

- **Location:** This is optional. Check the box, and enter descriptive text if you're forming a team specifically for Etsians in your geographical area.

- **Short Description**: This mandatory, brief passage appears with the team logo on its profile page.

- **Long Description:** This optional text, when entered, appears on the team's home page.

- **Who can join:** If you restrict membership, or require qualifications or information to join the team, add this option.

- **Team Access:** Indicates whether the team is Open (anyone can join) or Moderated (newcomers must apply).

- **Application Questions:** Include the application questions here if your team requires application for membership. Check the box to require applicants to answer a question. By leaving the box unchecked, you can make the answers voluntary.

- **Logo:** Use an appropriate image, 170 x 100 pixels.

- **Tags:** Provide keywords relevant to your team (your craft style, intended customers, location, etc.) Tags will help the right people find your team in searches.

- **Related Links:** Insert the address of other websites related to your team. Remember, it's against Etsy rules to push shoppers to an alternative sales venue. Furthermore, if the main purpose of your team is to promote a specific product, service, or outside website, you need to ask Etsy for permission beforehand. Send a message to teams@etsy.com.

Save your team's details by clicking **Create Team** at the bottom of the page.

Team discussion forums

Each team has a dedicated discussion board, similar to Etsy forums. They exist to post announcements, to air discussion and criticism, or to simply socialize. Posting messages is restricted to team members, but discussion threads may be public. Whoever starts a thread may specify that it's private (visible only to signed-in team members) or public (viewable by anyone online).

Team captains, along with any "leaders" they appoint, moderate the discussion. Responsibility for enforcing rules and removing inappropriate content rests with the team, not Etsy—although Etsy reserves the right to shut down teams who create problems for other members. Team forums are considered a public space, and subject to the same community policies as Etsy's regular discussion boards—in addition to team policies outlined by the captain.

Each team member is able to flag a post for removal. Team captains and leaders have editing links at the bottom of each post, enabling them to delete the post, close the topic, or contact the post author.

Here are some good, general rules for using and administering team discussion boards:

- **Give people the benefit of the doubt.** Don't accuse someone of rule-breaking without having the facts, or privately asking for an explanation beforehand.

- **Be kind.** Don't use discussion boards as a vehicle for embarrassing someone, or settling scores. If someone violates a policy, bring attention to the policy, not the person who violated it.

- **Use humor with great care.** What may seem hilarious to you could be highly offensive to someone else. Make yourself the butt of the jokes, and don't volunteer someone else as the scapegoat.

- **Be patient.** The bigger your team, the more likely disputes will arise, as well as seemingly repetitive and elementary discussions. Remember that you, too, were once a bright-eyed, bushy-tailed newcomer.

Using team tags

Just as you can use descriptive keywords to "tag" your item listings, Etsy teams have unique tags to enable shoppers to find items made by members of a given team.

If a team wants to use a team-specific item listing tag, it must include the word "team." Team can appear at the beginning, middle, or end of the tag.

Once you've decided on a team tag, announce it in your team's description so members will know which tag to use, and shoppers will know which tag to search for.

Etsy members who aren't on your team aren't supposed to use your team's tag, although it happens sometimes—not all Etsy sellers are familiar with the team program. If you discover a seller outside your team using your team tag, try sending a polite message requesting they delete the tag. If the issue can't be resolved, contact teams@etsy.com. Be sure to mention the user name of the person inappropriately using your tag, your team name and team tag, and how you've been unable to resolve the issue.

Etsy's Team Grants program

When a team's activities benefit the team and Etsy, the company rewards the team with monthly funding. Etsy has a team grants program it doles out once a month, based on the needs identified in team applications. The major criteria Etsy considers when awarding a grant are how much awareness of Etsy the team's activity will generate, and how much traffic it might bring to Etsy's site. Also, will the team's project publicize Etsy among a new audience in a creative, memorable way? Do the team members have a successful track record on Etsy, and is the group membership active and committed?

Typical grant winners include a group of sellers buying a newspaper or magazine advertisement showcasing their wares, or having the cost of attending an event or promotion subsidized. However, Etsy insists on prior approval of any advertising, and it doesn't want teams to imply that they're Etsy employees.

Teams can win up to two grants per calendar year. To learn all the rules about grants and perhaps apply, complete the form at this address: Etsy.com/teams/grant

If you win a team grant, Etsy will require you to file an expense report and document the project with a video, blog, or website. Etsy's staff wants to know how well your project fared, to help evaluate future grant applications.

Team accounts

Etsy teams sometime set up a "collective" account, where the team operates a seller account or a shopper account. Whoever registers for the account is responsible for all the activity from it.

Team shopper accounts. Having a shopper account enables you to generate an Etsy Mini for use on member blogs and websites. The Etsy Mini generated from the account's favorites can serve as a marketing vehicle for your team's shops. You can sell team items to help pay for advertising and team activities.

Having a team shopper account requires an email address dedicated to the team, with a secure password you can distribute to other team members.

Team shops

Team shops can sell items donated by team members, or items made collaboratively. A successful Etsy shop is a big undertaking, so it's prudent to have a longstanding, trusting relationship with all team members. Among the team tasks:

• Registering a credit card with Etsy to pay bills generated by the account. Usually, an individual's card is used for the account, since Etsy Teams rarely have joint bank accounts. If an Etsy team isn't a licensed business, then the individual who registers the card is responsible for payments, fees, and any late penalties incurred with the account.

• Deciding each member's role in the shop, and indicating this on the public profile.

• Forming policies on how payments are accepted, and exactly how the money is handled after receipt.

• Having a backup plan for shipping and administering the account if a team member can't meet his or her responsibilities. Each team member should have complete contact information for all persons involved.

• Disclosing all members with access to the shop account in the shop profile, and ensuring members disclose this access in their individual shops, too.

• Following all of Etsy's rules with your team account. For example, you can't buy items from a team shop for which you have password access. This is considered "shilling," or buying from yourself.

For questions about teams, contact Etsy's staff at teams@etsy.com.

Online labs and Livestream

Not everyone has the time or opportunity to attend crafting classes or marketing seminars. Fortunately, Etsy sponsors a series of interactive online labs through an Internet video service called Livestream. You can type in questions during the live events or ask questions orally if your computer is equipped with a microphone.

Using Livestream, you can browse the schedule of upcoming Etsy-sponsored events and register for them. You can also view recordings of previous labs. To see a listing of events and instructions on accessing them, visit the "Community" tab on Etsy, then click Online Labs.

Crafting at Etsy Labs, the company's headquarters and creative space in Brooklyn, N.Y. Weekly craft nights feature knitting, photography, screen-printing, bicycle repair, and much more. If you're not in Brooklyn, Etsy's virtual labs come to you—an interactive menu of crafting workshops and selling tutorials at **Livestream.com/etsy**.

Seller Profile: Villa de la Lega

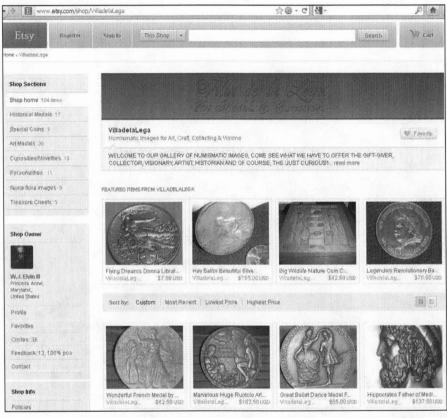

W.J. Elvin III of Princess Anne, Md., is a dealer in "imaginology" as he applies it to art medals and other curiosities. He collects and sells medals, unique coins, and certain tokens, mostly for the artistic images they offer. Unlike some coin dealers, he doesn't "grade" coins, nor value them for precious metal. Instead, he researches their historic value, their irony, their mystery, and sometimes humor, often unintended.
See Etsy.com/shop/VilladelaLega

How did you get involved with art medals and numismatic curiosities, and how do you find them?

When I was a youngster my grandfather would sometimes take me to Mr. Cessna's cubby-hole coin shop in the old mountain town of Cumberland, Md., down a narrow Dickensian side street. It was a dazzling experience for me, and I would leave clutching an Indian Head penny or some other small

treasure. I've been a treasure hunter ever since, though these days I am more likely to prowl the Internet rather than sticks-and-bricks shops, or flea markets and garage sales.

The only buying secret, for me, is to spend an inordinate amount of time visiting the auction sites and other sales venues—looking, looking, looking for that special item. Most people don't have time for that sort of thing, so I suppose I'm a surrogate searcher for customers who share my interests.

Legendary Revolutionary Bandit Francisco Pancho Villa

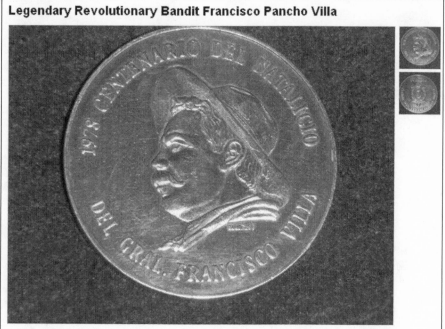

ρ zoom

1978, signed Alvarado.

Francisco Pancho Villa was leader of an outlaw band, charming and ruthless, he joined the 1910 Mexican revolution and recruited thousands to the cause including many from the U.S. In some ways he lived up to his Robin Hood image, dividing up huge ranches among widows and relations of his soldiers and followers.

As a celebrity, he staged battles for U.S. newspaper correspondents. He later provoked punitive expeditions from the U.S. due to raids across the border.

Villa's real name was Doroteo Arango and he supposedly had 26 official marriages which might be so -- if you visited Durango and adjacent northern Mexico some years ago there seemed a Pancho Villa widow welcoming tourists at every turn, so to speak.

I believe this medal bears the mintmark of the Durango official mint. It was sold as an ounce of silver though I have no way to test it.

Villa was given a military pension to settle him down and he was assassinated in 1923.

There are many legends, the stuff of books and movies.

The medal is an inch and one half across.

Generally the best art medals of the golden era, say 1880 to 1930, come from Belgium and France.

Do you sell on other online marketplaces, and how do you like Etsy?

I will try to sell elsewhere if the item doesn't fit with what I'm trying to do on Etsy, which is to offer unique images to a public that may be unfamiliar with art medals or even numismatics in general. I want to reach the artist, the seeker, anyone who might be inspired by the images on these little handheld sculptures. Or sometimes I just want to amuse or entertain. Etsy is a wonderful place for that, an exotic bazaar rather than a rigid sales site. I have met the most wonderful people there, as often inquisitive as acquisitive.

How do you attract customers and get repeat business?

Etsy brings people my way through devices such as Circles, Favorites, Treasuries and the search engine. As a somewhat retired journalist, I still blog and am working on a variety of articles that will help publicize the Etsy shop. As for repeats, I really do want people to find what they are seeking, and will help in any way I can, time permitting. These people remember that they were treated as a friend rather than as a credit card number.

What is your procedure for valuing and pricing your items?

That's tricky. Interestingly, there are no price guides for art medals, not that price guides are much good anyway. With art medals, you really have to tune your intuition, as well as learn the history of the field—who the great medallists were, and so on.

Your items are so unique; do you have any competitors on Etsy?

The field is vast, and often there are few of a particular art medal available. A mint run of only a thousand is not unusual. So although there are others who offer art medals, we are not often competing item by item. I doubt if there's any other seller so focused on the image, so Jungian about what they sell. To me, "what does it say?" is of far greater importance than "what is it worth monetarily?" and I hope to reach like-minded people.

Your biggest job must be researching your items and describing them in an interesting way. How do you do it?

I have experience in magazine feature writing. These days I'm doing what I love to do. The research, whether it's reading books or asking experts, is a real pleasure. And I get a kick out of presenting the item and its story in a way that can attract people—no mean feat, considering the blizzard of information bombarding us today.

Have you ever bought something for resale, then decided you couldn't part with it?

I don't buy things thinking, "Oh, someone will pay a lot for that." Usually, what I buy has set off bells and whistles in my psyche. I want to study it further, find meaning in it, savor the irony of it, or perhaps enjoy the features of a lovely lady—from an artistic perspective, of course.

I'm not a hoarder, I like to share treasures. But yes, there are a few keepers, images with special meaning for me.

At the moment I'm looking at a tray of about 40 medallic images of horses— race horses, rodeo horses, war horses, and so on. I am enjoying their company, but I also know that one day they will gallop off to the Etsy corral for resale.

PUT GOOGLE TO WORK FOR YOU

Would you like to boost your customer base, sell more of your creations, and earn more money—without spending a dime on advertising or computer-geek experts? I thought so—just keep reading. Search Engine Optimization, or SEO, is a series of techniques for boosting the visibility of your shop and listings, and thereby attracting sales. Like everything we've discussed to this point, there's an art to it, and a science, too.

First, we'll examine some simple, but powerful, SEO techniques you can apply within the confines of Etsy. Then we'll learn to improve your visibility not only on Google, but Yahoo, Bing.com, and every other website that helps people find information. Once you get the knack of this, you'll be attracting buyers who've never heard of you OR Etsy. You'll even be getting sales from people who weren't even shopping in the first place!

Some people will try to persuade you that SEO is something you need to "buy." If you let them, Internet consultants will charge you an arm and a leg for SEO advice. They'll promise the moon: the "first page" on Google. They'll argue that SEO is too complicated, too "techie" for normal people. Their come-ons work just like any other get-rich-quick scheme—they take money from suckers. Take a good look at their offers, and you'll notice there's no money-back guarantee. The reason? SEO is like word of mouth. If you bought it, it's probably not going to work. But if it happens because you're loving what you're doing, then it's golden.

And that's the bottom line: You know your business and your customer better than anyone. Word of mouth, the best advertising, is something you can't buy. It's something that happens because of the commitment you made from Day One—simply making good stuff, and standing behind it.

Yes, it's simple: SEO is a series of simple concepts you can learn and apply yourself. Yes, ethical, decent behavior has just rewards. Concentrating on making great crafts, and selling them professionally, striving for excellence, following the simple instructions in this book, produces results.

SEO on Etsy: browsing vs. searching

Etsy is a great place to shop and browse. Just as when they're wandering through a giant shopping mall filled with unique stores, Etsy shoppers love to stumble upon things, browsing through categories and lists of favorites, clicking through "favorites," and poking through shops. Serendipity is fun. But most purchases, on Etsy and everywhere else, are no accident. Most shoppers have a good idea of what they want. They're searching for something. SEO helps ensure that if shoppers are looking for what you've got, they'll find you.

When a buyer searches for something on Etsy, the default method is "relevancy." Using the drop-down menu, searchers can then sort the search results according to the most-recent listings, highest-price listings, and lowest-price items.

So "relevancy" is key; it's making things obvious. By following some simple rules, your listings will be as obvious as possible, rising to the top of Etsy's search results. Your creations will be easier for shoppers to find, and much more likely to be bought.

Here are a few rules of thumb for enhancing the relevancy of your listings. Understand these concepts, and you'll rank higher within Etsy searches:

- **Provide accurate, descriptive titles <u>with important words at the beginning.</u>** Etsy gives listing titles the most weight in search results. And Etsy gives more weight to the words toward the beginning of your listing. So, ensure that the first few words explain what the item is. For example, let's imagine someone is searching for an "evening gown," and you're selling one. Your listing for "Wool Evening Gown, Black & White Lace" will rank high in the search results. By contrast, if you'd titled the same listing "One-Shoulder Wool Lace, Black & White Fantasy Evening Gown," you'll be way down at the bottom of the results, and probably go unnoticed.

- **Recency:** On Etsy, recent listings (items listed for sale within the past few days, instead of weeks or months ago) are more likely to be exposed to shoppers. Recency is most important when a search turns up lots of competing listings. For example, let's imagine a shopper uses a very broad search term, like "bag." In cases like this, Etsy will return more than 100,000 listings, and give added weight toward newer listings. This advantage given recent listings is why sellers who list in hotly competitive categories will often cancel and relist items after a few days, even though the listing is effective for 120 days. They prefer to pay the 20-cent listing fee rather than see their listings become buried in search results by more recent listings. It all depends on how unusual—or routine—your items are.

For example, if you're one of only a handful of sellers with "dog-tooth earrings" then you're not going to get buried by new listings. Your listings will be plainly visible until they expire in 120 days, as long as someone searches for "dog-tooth earrings."

- **Keywords, keywords, keywords.** There's an old saying in real estate: "The three most important things are 'location, location and location.'" For an online business, the three biggies are "keywords, keywords and keywords." Keywords are everything. Without the right keywords, you're invisible, no matter what kind of real estate you've got. Find the right keywords, and it's like your Etsy listings will be on Fifth Avenue or Rodeo Drive.

How do you find the best keywords? Put yourself in the place of the shopper. Look for something similar to what you're selling. Which listings bubble to the top in a search? Figure out why.

The best keywords depend entirely on what you're selling. But here are some hints: Use concrete words, such as "Bowtie," "Rhinestone," and "Patent leather." Now, here's what keywords are NOT: "whimsy" or imprecise words like "Magical" or "Misty memory," or worn-out adjectives like "super." Unless you're selling Superman, "super" is not a keyword. Keywords are the words shoppers will type in to find something they want to buy—"towel," "necklace," and "candle holder."

And remember, keywords aren't confined to your listings—they're crucial to your Shop Title and Shop Announcement, too. Key the right keywords in there, and they're shopper magnets. If your business or line of merchandise changes, then it's time to reevaluate the keywords in your Shop Title and Shop Announcement.

- **Enclose a short description within your tags.** Accurate, descriptive tags are another way to optimize your listings, and Etsy has an additional search feature that prioritizes listings with precise word pairings. For example, if someone searches for "red corvette," results that contain "red corvette" in the listing title or tags will usually appear higher in search results compared with a listing titled "red vintage car corvette" and without the tag "red corvette."

- **Don't use the same old tags on every listing.** Take the time to dream up just the right tags for each item, which will expose your items to more shoppers.

Find more keywords, better keywords

Nobody knows more about keywords than Google. You can use the company's free keyword research tool by visiting this address:

https://adwords.google.com/select/KeywordToolExternal.

Google's free keyword tool reveals keyword ideas related to the search terms you enter. In the example above, the search phrase is "pearl necklace." Sometimes you can gain more traffic by using more uncommon keyword combinations. With less competition for that phrase, you have a better chance of being noticed in search results. Google's tool could also reveal effective keyword combinations that didn't occur to you while you drafted your item description.

You can click Advanced options to further refine your search according to country, language, or mobile users.

Etsy shop stats

You can get valuable insight into how Etsy shoppers are searching for and finding your listings by studying the "Shop Stats" section of Your Shop > Shop Stats in the "Orders" section. The "dashboard" shows data on views, favorites, orders, and revenue, and three reports revealing how visitors find your shop:

1. **Top Traffic Sources.** Websites that sent visitors to your shop.

2. **Top Traffic Sources on Etsy.** Etsy pages and features that visitors viewed before coming to your shop.

3. **Top Keywords.** The words people used to find your shop using Etsy's search and other search tools.

When you first log in, Shop Stats shows data for the past week, but you can change the view to today, yesterday, last 30 days, or a specific range of dates.

SEO for the Web

OK, we've discussed some techniques for making our Etsy shop and listings easier to find. These next steps will raise our profile everywhere—on Etsy, and at search engines like Google, Yahoo, and Bing.

• Have unique products that sell themselves

This one is obvious, but it's true. On Etsy or your own Web store, to be the cream of the crop, you must create products that virtually sell themselves.

You can't survive on Etsy by trying to sell cookie-cutter products. To succeed, your inventory must be unique, eye-catching, attractive items that scream, "Buy me now! I'm not available anywhere else!" You've got make good products, create inviting, professional-looking listings for them, and do it consistently over time. Whether you're a new crafter or a grizzled veteran, this niche approach is a good recipe for success at Etsy (and SEO). You won't conquer Amazon, Nordstrom's, and Cartier in your first week.

• Refining your Shop Title and Announcement

Potential customers are looking at your Shop Title and Announcement every day. When was the last time you had a good gander at this yourself? If it needs polishing, edit your Title and Announcement by visiting Your Account > Info & Appearance.

Shop Title. This is the first text someone sees on Google or other search tools that link to your shop. Only about 66 characters, including spaces, are picked up, so every character is precious. On the Google results, only the first 48 characters appear on the top, hyperlinked line—your title is truncated, and your user name is included at the end of the line.

Use this page to briefly describe your shop and what you're selling. Should your real name, or business name, be part of your page title? Sure—if you're famous, and people search for your name. Most of us are better off just saying what we're selling.

Shop Announcement. The beginning of this text, the first 160 characters, is what people see underneath the title of your shop page. In Internet parlance, this is called the "meta description." Here's your chance to make sure the right people click, and visit your shop. Continue explaining your shop and what you sell, working in more of the keywords shoppers are likely to use when searching for items like yours.

Sharpen your Shop sections

Continue the same pattern in your Shop Sections, another element of your shop's SEO. Each section has its own "landing" page with a page title drawn from the section name. Edit these by visiting Your Account > Info & Appearance > Sections. Use concrete words, keywords, such as "Dresses," "Handbags," and "Flannel" for your Sections. Don't use whimsical, stylish terms like "Afternoon delights" or "Unbelievable finds." Use the words people use when searching for something specific—"originals," "prints," "watercolors."

Optimize your item descriptions

Just as your shop announcement serves as the meta description of your shop, your item description comprises the meta description of that listing page. It's what people see under the hyperlinked page title if they find your item page in Google search results.

Sure, you already know what an "item description" is. But think about it some more. Here's where you drill down into exactly what this item is. Don't regurgitate what's already on your Shop Announcement, because you want the item page to be **different**—to be highly visible on the Internet, the page has to be **specific and relevant** to the item. You don't get extra credit for boilerplate, you get penalized.

Only the first 160 characters appear in search results, although the entire description is indexed by Google, so certain keywords, even at the bottom, can bring results. But mostly, the first 160 characters are what most people will see in Google results, and it's how they'll decide whether your page is worth visiting. So, now you know how important it is, when writing your item descriptions, to get down to brass tacks immediately. Describe your item briefly in the first sentence. Be sure to let people know that this is something they can buy now, not just read about. Then add secondary details.

If you've got great keywords, they're worth repeating. That helps Google determine that your page is truly relevant to those search terms. But don't go nuts. If you repeat yourself more than a couple times, Google will decide your page is "spam" and ignore it. Little tricks like this are part of Google's "secret sauce," how it decides which pages are "interesting" and worth showing. It's literally a secret formula, an algorithm.

Nobody outside Google's headquarters knows its search algorithm, the precise calculations it uses to decide which pages are "interesting" and worth showing first. We only know some rules of thumb. Your pages should be unique, have consistent keywords, and have incoming links from a variety of websites.

Building links to your Etsy pages

OK, we've discussed how to optimize your shop and listings for searching. Now, we'll reinforce that work by building links to your Etsy shops. Two simple, effective ways to build links are by using an Etsy Mini, and by posting comments to the Etsy blog and forums.

Etsy Mini

If you have a Facebook page—or a blog or website—Etsy Mini is a handy tool for displaying items from your shop. To use this tool, visit **Your Account >** Etsy Mini (it's in the sidebar, under the Promote heading).

The top row of your Mini displays your featured listings, and descending rows show recently listed items. You can adjust the width of a Mini to display as many as four items in each row.

Another option is to use a Mini to display your favorites, and it will display the most recently hearted items. You can rearrange the order within a Mini.

Once you adjust the Mini to your liking, you can copy the automatically generated HTML code and paste it into your site, instantly building a series of links to your Etsy pages.

You may need to check the help section of your blogging service or consult your Web designer if you're not familiar with how to alter the code of your website.

Commenting at Etsy blogs and forums. Contribute to the Etsy blog, Etsy.com/blog, by posting comments when you have something interesting to add to the discussion. Adding your own comments to the official Etsy blog allows you to build internal links to your Etsy shop or website.

SELLER PROFILE: The Silver Diva

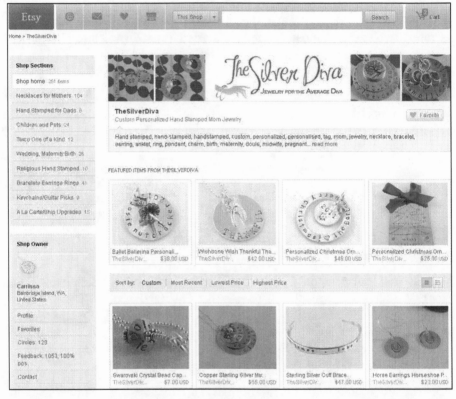

Carrissa Barbee of Bainbridge Island, Wash., is proprietor of The Silver Diva, which sells personalized hand-stamped jewelry on Etsy, eBay, Artfire, eCrater, and a stand-alone site. See **Etsy.com/shop/thesilverdiva.**

How did you get started?

I am an attorney by trade and needed to find another way to make money and stay home with my children. So when my second child was born seven years ago, I decided to quit my attorney job and sell jewelry. Originally I was traveling to Taxco, Mexico, to look for fine hand-crafted sterling silver and sell it at trade shows, fundraisers and other events. With my second pregnancy, I could no longer attend all the shows, so I had to find a way to unload all of my inventory. I started on eBay, and after I sold off all my inventory, I began thinking of other ways to sell jewelry from home. I taught myself how to hand-stamp, and it took off from there.

How has your business evolved since you started, and how have you managed the economic climate?

Since I started hand stamping a couple of years ago, my business has doubled. We started it basically on Etsy, and then threw in product line also onto eBay, eCrater, ArtFire, and most recently, I started my own website, The-Silver-Diva.com. This year has been the busiest thus far, and we will have sales well over $100,000.

It has not been a tough economic climate in jewelry. I would say that jewelry never suffers. It's a relatively small purchase that women often indulge to make themselves feel better, so it doesn't seem to suffer like other industries.

What is your creative process?

I look around at what other vendors are creating, and try to think outside the box about what I would personally like to wear. We also specialize in birth and maternity jewelry, which is hard to find, so that is a really fun avenue to explore.

How do you attract customers and get repeat business?

We continually renew on Etsy several times a day to get our items to the front. We have a Facebook fan page and a Twitter [account.] This year in June, we ran a Groupon [online deal-of-the-day coupon] in Seattle for Father's Day. We participate in a ton of blog giveaways to publicize us. Also, this year we began advertising in magazines: *Martha Stewart Weddings, Martha Stewart Living*, and *Real Simple*.

We also do online advertising through Facebook, Google Adwords, and Theknot.com.

What percentage of your business is online?

At this point, 99.9 percent of our business is online. We stopped doing all trade shows. We do have some product sold in stores via wholesale, but it's a very small percentage. Hand-stamped jewelry is extremely fashionable right now and I think this will continue for a long time. It's not the same as engraving, but a wonderful alternative, and engraving will never leave!

It's good also that the indie movement is so big right now.

How do you price your items?

We take our product cost and multiply it by three. For some sites that have big fees, we add the fees to calculate the total price.

Circle Birthstone Custom Personalized Sterling Silver Necklace

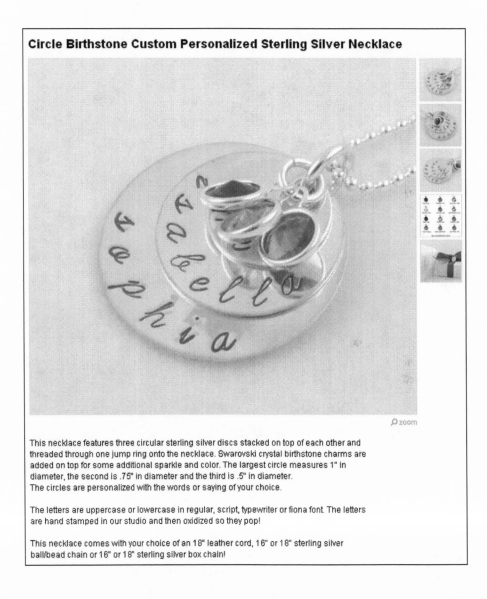

$\mathcal{P}$ zoom

This necklace features three circular sterling silver discs stacked on top of each other and threaded through one jump ring onto the necklace. Swarovski crystal birthstone charms are added on top for some additional sparkle and color. The largest circle measures 1" in diameter, the second is .75" in diameter and the third is .5" in diameter. The circles are personalized with the words or saying of your choice.

The letters are uppercase or lowercase in regular, script, typewriter or fiona font. The letters are hand stamped in our studio and then oxidized so they pop!

This necklace comes with your choice of an 18" leather cord, 16" or 18" sterling silver ball/bead chain or 16" or 18" sterling silver box chain!

PAYING TO ADVERTISE YOUR ETSY SHOP

We've looked at various ways you can promote your Etsy business the smart way—for free. Many successful Etsy sellers never exhaust the free promotional opportunities.

Now we're entering the realm of paid advertising. And paid advertising carries with it some risk. To put it plainly, if you spend a lot of money on advertising without knowing what you're doing, you can easily go broke.

The collective wisdom among many experienced Etsy sellers who've tried paid advertising in various forms—Etsy's Showcase, search ads, or outside programs like Google Adwords or Facebook ads—is that advertising rarely pays off. And that's the bottom line: If you're paying to advertise your Etsy business, the goal is to earn more money than was possible without the advertising.

For most Etsy sellers offering items at $15 to $25 apiece, most paid advertising programs just don't work. What really works is "free advertising," also known as word of mouth. But you can't buy word-of-mouth. You must earn it by compiling a track record of sales and customer feedback—by offering great items and making your customers so happy, they'll recommend you to others.

Yes, your advertising dollars may bring in a couple of hundred shoppers, but that pales in comparison to the "free" business you'll have coming your way if you focus on making great items and keeping your customers happy.

Here are some caveats about using Etsy Search Ads, the showcase, or any other paid advertising program:

- **Don't pay for advertising before your Etsy business is up and running for at least one year.** First, you must understand your customer base, how they find you, and how they decide to buy from you instead of someone else. You've got to know your costs, what a customer is worth to you, and how much you can afford to pay for ads. Remember, many wildly successful Etsy sellers don't advertise at all—they've got all the business they can handle. Their customers happily do their advertising for them—through good feedback and word of mouth.

- **Be patient.** If sales are slow, especially in the beginning, it's tempting to plop down a wad of cash for ads. For a moment, buying ads feels great; it feels like you're taking bold action to jump-start your business. In reality, there probably are other reasons that sales are slow—your items aren't in demand, your listings don't sparkle, your customer base isn't big enough yet, the niche you're targeting is oversupplied. Businesses never starve from lack of advertising; they die from a lack of customers. Part of the fees and commissions you're paying Etsy is for exposure. For a while, think of that as your advertising. You're paying to sell on Etsy, and Etsy's end of the bargain is delivering some customers for you. If you're spending a lot to drive customers to Etsy, you're doing part of Etsy's job for it.

- **Pay only for what you can measure.** If you're going to pay for advertising, pay only for what you can measure. Know exactly how many sales your advertising dollars are bringing in. Is your profit margin less than $20 or $30 per item, like most sellers? Then your sales are unlikely to pay for any advertising that will make a noticeable difference in your sales. This simple rule, "pay for what you can measure," applies to any type of advertising where you can't track the sales produced directly from the ad. For example, if you pay $100 for a weekly newspaper ad, and you don't know how many sales it produces, that money might be wasted. On the other hand, if you create a special coupon discount code which appears in that newspaper ad, and you can count the amount of sales and profit resulting from those sales, then you'll know whether the ad is working. Likewise, if you pay $50 a week for a banner ad on a website, it might result in thousands of views or "impressions" but no measurable sales. If, on the other hand, you know how many times people actually click on the ad, and how often those clicks result in a sale, you can measure your results. This is why many folks who advertise on the Internet prefer "pay per click" ad systems, like Google Adwords. It can be impossible to evaluate the results of other ad systems, where you pay for a certain amount of "impressions" the ad gets. Sure, the Web page might have been viewed by a million people, but how many people actually paid attention to your ad, or purchased something after seeing it?

The approach advocated in this book is to think of Etsy as a selling platform with "training wheels." It's a ready-made marketplace with a low barrier to entry. It's much easier to get started on Etsy compared with the alternatives, like starting your own website or lugging your merchandise to craft fairs on weekends.

But that doesn't mean you'll necessarily be satisfied with doing business exclusively on Etsy over the long term. Many Etsy sellers who think big— those who have a long-range plan to earn a living from their craft—have plans to "graduate" from Etsy. That means to transition to a sales platform they own and have exclusive control over—their own website, a shop, consignment sales, perhaps licensing their designs. Does that mean they're abandoning Etsy? Not at all. As long as Etsy is providing value for the fees paid, is generating new customers and happy experiences, Etsy might keep you busy indefinitely. It might become a small component of your business, or a linchpin. It's up to you, where you see the best opportunity to achieve your goals.

In any event, advertising is a whole new can of worms. It's an investment. It's risk. And whenever you're making a big investment, you must have YOUR bottom line ruling your decision-making. And that's why you can't do paid advertising at first—you don't even know what your bottom line is yet!

It's sad but true: A lot of advertising—perhaps most small ad buys—are sold to suckers whose money is wasted. If you're risking your money, make sure you're getting results for your dollars.

Can paid advertising work with an Etsy-based business? Of course it can. But it's most likely to work when you have an established business with two key characteristics:

- **High price points and high profit margins.** If your items sell for $100 or $200, and your profit margins exceed 40 percent, you might be able to make the advertising pay. It's possible. If your price points are about $20, forget it.

- **A proven customer list.** Let's say you've been in business for four years. You've got a customer list of about 1,000 who spend an average of $250 with you, year after year. Those are repeat customers. Now you should have some cash you can risk toward advertising because you know that acquiring a new customer brings in an average $250 in sales annually.

Display yourself with Showcase

Showcase is an in-house Etsy advertising tool you can use to increase exposure of your items and shop. Multiple Showcases exist for various Etsy categories and subcategories.

To buy a one-day spot on the Showcase, visit the Showcase Gateway by visiting Your Shop > Showcase (in the sidebar under the Promotion heading.) Click the Book a Slot button.

Select one of the available Showcases for various Etsy categories and subcategories and an available time slot. Remember that some Showcases are restricted to certain categories, tags, and themes.

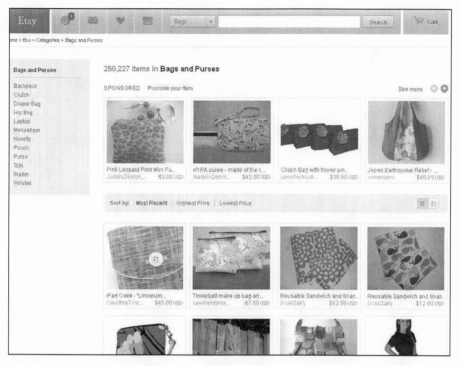

Browsing in the "Bags and Purses" category. The top row of "sponsored" listings are Showcase placements.

Showcases are displayed in a module atop matching category pages. They include listings from 25 sellers each day. A one-day spot costs $7.

Each spot in a Showcase has a queue of item listings. By default, when you buy a Showcase spot, 10 of your shop's recently listed items are added to the queue. Also, you can manually rearrange your Showcase queue by visiting Your Account > Showcase. You can delete item listings, or add new ones by entering the listing ID and clicking Add. You can rearrange the order by using the Up and Down buttons.

Etsy Search Ads

A key to success with Etsy is refining your listings until they sparkle and virtually sell themselves. But regardless of how wonderful your items might be and how professional your listings are, a buyer has to SEE your listing before you get a sale. Showing up on the first page of search results helps tremendously, but it's nearly impossible if you're in a crowded niche.

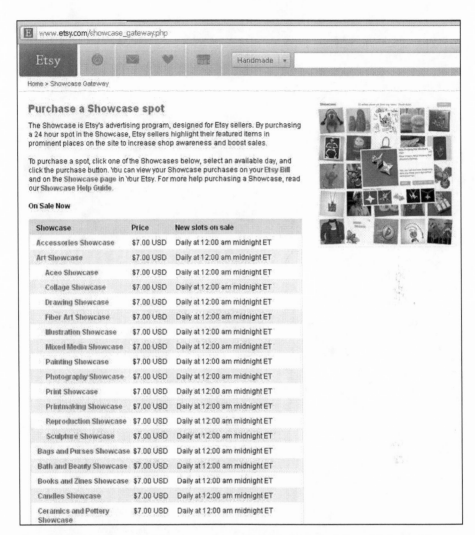

A potential answer to this conundrum is Etsy Search Ads, which enable you to buy your way to the top of search results -- literally. You simply decide which items in your shop you want to promote, select the keywords you want to pay for, and set a weekly budget of as little as $5. You can advertise your whole shop, or just certain items.

The more you pay, the more people will see your ads. However, that exposure doesn't automatically translate into sales or profits. Just because your ad appears doesn't mean someone will click on it, or buy your item.

You can buy Search Ads by looking under the Promote link in the left sidebar of Your Shop. Click Search Ads.

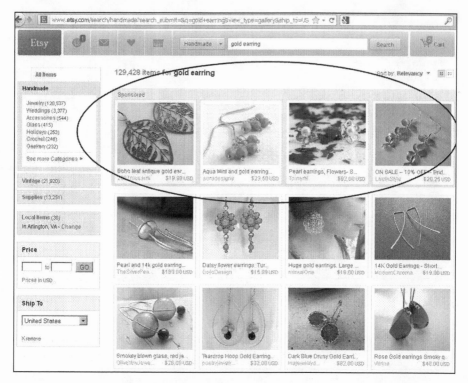

An Etsy keyword search for 'gold earring' produces a row of 'Sponsored' listings on the top row. These listings are highlighted on top because the shop owners bought Search Ads for the keyword phrase 'gold earring.' Each time an ad appears, it's counted as an 'impression.' If someone clicks on the ad to view the listing, it's counted as a 'view.'

After you buy Search Ads, the ads begin appearing at 12 p.m. GMT, or Greenwich Mean Time. GMT is a time reference that doesn't change with seasons. Compare Greenwich Mean Time to your local time by visiting http://wwp.greenwichmeantime.com.

Search Ads may be purchased in a seven-day block. You can review the dates and cost of your ad campaign before paying. When you sign up for Search Ads, Etsy will suggest some keywords that shoppers are searching for most often, and match them with your items, according to your tags and item titles.

You'll receive a weekly report from Etsy detailing each item's views and performance with various keywords. The Search Ad report you receive will detail the total cost of the ads, along with the number of impressions, views (when someone clicks on your ad) and the resulting Favorites adds, orders, and revenue.

You can focus on promoting all your items, or a particular group of items. If you decide to stop promoting a certain item during the week, you can turn off individual items mid-week. If a promoted listing is sold, deactivated, or expires during the week, Etsy will stop showing ads for that item and refocus your ad funding on other items in your shop.

Search Ads use the primary photo you've uploaded for an item, so it's essential to have a stunning item photo to draw interest. You'll be competing against good sellers who also are risking their money on Search Ads.

Etsy Search Ads is an "impression"-based advertising system. The average cost is about $1.20 per 1,000 impressions. Each time your promoted item is displayed at the top of the page for an Etsy shopper, it's counted as an impression. Of course, an "impression" doesn't necessarily mean you get any result. Search Ad impressions don't indicate someone has clicked on your ad, merely that it was shown.

Remember that each time you perform a search using your ad campaign's keywords, you pay for the impression when your ad appears.

Etsy Search Ads are relatively new, so undoubtedly the program's performance will change over the next few years. In any case, sellers who have tested the ads and publicly reported their results in Etsy's Forums have reported similar results. The figures below represent typical performance of a Search Ads campaign per $100 spent to advertise relatively low-cost items priced at about $10:

$100 in Search Ads paid

Impressions = 78,442

Views (clicks) = 481

Favorites = 51

Orders = 14

So, each view costs about 21 cents, and each order costs about $7. Is that a good result? Well, it all depends on whether you have enough profit margin within your average order to pay $7 in advertising fees. Not likely, if your item is priced around $10.

Let's consider a different scenario: What if you're using Search Ads to promote items at a different price point, say $50? Would you still get the same level of response, 14 orders per $100 in advertising? Perhaps not, because customers resist higher prices, generally speaking. What if you could break even? If your ads consumed your entire profit on new customers, could you live with that? Your ads wouldn't result in instant profits, but your business would likely expand over the long term. Why? A certain percentage of those new customers would become repeat buyers. Another consideration: Some of the favorites resulting from your Search Ads should result in sales, perhaps weeks or months later. If you'd already broken even, these additional orders would be pure gravy.

It's clear that Etsy Search Ads might become a valuable opportunity for sellers who have the patience to test their results with different items at different price points, while using different keywords over an extended period of time—and then carefully evaluate their results. Sellers who half-heartedly commit $5 for a one-week ad campaign, then quickly become discouraged and drop the program, won't gain any insight.

Because Etsy Search Ads are relatively new, it's impossible to predict how viable they'll be for individual sellers. Etsy will undoubtedly enhance the program after a while, which may improve performance. On the other hand, if the ads prove popular among sellers, Etsy will probably raise the rates on Search Ads to increase the company's profits.

Another wild card: What will be the long-term response of Etsy buyers to the Search Ads? Perhaps the ads are getting lots of attention now because they're relatively new. Over time, if Etsy's customer base believes that Search Ads are helpful, then they'll click on them and buy more items. On the other hand, if Etsy customers believe Search Ads are irrelevant and annoying, they'll begin ignoring them and sales will suffer. Whatever the outcome, it will be fascinating to watch it unfold.

Google Adwords

The major alternative to Etsy Search Ads is Google Adwords. If you've ever used the Google search engine, you've probably seen the small advertisements that appear alongside the results.

Compared with Etsy Search Ads, the major difference with Google Adwords is that it's pay-per-click, or PPC, instead of Etsy's CPM, or cost-per-thousand impressions. Some advertising veterans like Google's system better because you only pay when someone clicks your ad. You're not paying anything for the thousands of people who ignore the ad.

The downside with Google Adwords, as with all advertising, is that you can burn through hundreds or thousands of dollars on ads.

Google search results for 'gold earring.' On the top and right sidebar are Adwords ads, and on the bottom-left corner are 'organic' search results, which appear based on the authority of the website and keyword matching.

Every cent might be wasted. That's because it can take dozens, perhaps hundreds, of ad clicks before someone buys your item. If you're paying Google a dollar or two for each click, which is common, you're unlikely to sell enough merchandise to pay for the ads—especially if you're the typical Etsy seller, whose items sell for $15 to $25 apiece. There's just not enough profit margin in a $20 item to pay for $30 worth of Google ads, no matter how you slice it. Most sellers are better off spending their time and energy taking advantage of the "free advertising" opportunities discussed throughout this book. By constantly improving their item photos, listing descriptions, keywords, and social marketing participation, skillful sellers can get all the business they can handle. You'll have the best "free" advertising on Earth—word of mouth from happy customers. Then you can concentrate on raking in the business, and let others pay the Adwords bills.

SELLER PROFILE: Lizbeth's Garden

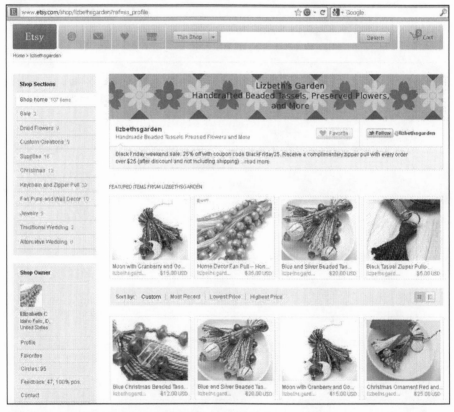

Elizabeth Cogliati of Idaho Falls, Idaho, is proprietor of Lizbeth's Garden. She specializes in handmade tassels, taking some thread and beads and turning them into a beautiful tassel. She also arranges dried flowers and potpourri sachets as a way of sharing the beauty of her garden. See **Etsy.com/shop/lizbethsgarden**.

How did you get started?

A few years ago, I decided to redecorate my bedroom. For months, I collected blue decor—curtains, tiebacks, a painting, a bedspread. I tucked it away and dreamed of the blue I would paint over the dingy white walls. But one thing I couldn't find: a new tassel fan pull for the fan. I didn't want mustard yellow, I wanted dark blue. With beads.

I visited store after store, catalog after catalog. Nobody had beaded tassel fan pulls, at any price.

Painting day came. The artwork was hung, the curtains were up, the new bedspread was on the bed. And still, no fan pull. Sadly, I attached the blue glass fan pull I'd found at a big-box store.

Months later, I found a book with instructions for making beaded tassels for pillows. I figured out how to make the tassels and attach a fan pull chain instead, and Lizbeth's Garden was born—a place where you can shop for all kinds of tassels—fan pulls, purse tassels, tiny earrings, and everything in between.

Then what happened?

Instead of making just one size and type of beaded tassels, I decided to make four sizes, and now I make everything from jewelry to wall hangings. I also sell dried flowers, potpourri, custom metal medallions, art collages, and other home decor items.

How do you design your pieces?

For a beaded tassel, I start with a bead or beads that catch my eye. I match them with thread, then decide what kind of tassel to make, based on what I feel will sell (or is selling) in my online store. Then I get started.

Where do your customers come from?

I carry business cards wherever I go. For local, in-person business, I rely on word of mouth. For online sales, I promote via my blog and Twitter. I also belong to an amazing Etsy team, the Etsy DListers, whose members promote and support each other.

What's your mix of online and offline sales?

My business is 50 percent in-person and 50 percent online. In the spring and summer, I have more business in-person. In fall and winter, I have more online business.

How do you arrive at prices?

I price my items by adding up the cost of materials, then multiplying by my profit margin factor. I make sure my prices are high enough so that I can have a promotional sale, or sell wholesale, while still making a profit. For items that are extremely time-consuming, over two hours of creation time, I also add in an hourly wage for myself.

What's your take on paid advertising? Have you tried Google Ad-words, or blog ads?

I've never tried Google AdWords. I've bought display advertising in blog sidebars, in the sidebar of a site that provides analytics for Etsy sellers (not Google). And once I bought into an advertising co-op for crafters. I usually saw my views in my Etsy store increase the day or the week the advertising started, then gradually decrease back to normal by the end of the ad run. I never got a single sale I could attribute to the advertising.

Pink Beaded Tassel Wedding Bling or Valentine's Day Ornament

$\mathcal{P}$ zoom

This cute and flirty pink beaded tassel is the perfect way to say 'I love you.' Give it as a Valentine's Day gift, or decorate your wedding bouquet with it.

It is also just right for your ring pillow, boutonniere, corsage, or centerpiece.

I can make more than one, just ask.

Want this tassel in a different size, color or with a different top? Contact me for a custom order to match your wedding colors (matching pearls may not be available in all colors). Keychain tops also available for the perfect wedding favor. Match your wedding colors exactly when you buy a thread and bead sample: http://www.etsy.com/listing/78179720 /thread-and-bead-color-sample

What about Etsy Search Ads?

I tried them, and for my shop the results were miserable. The system wouldn't allow me to use the most popular search terms people use to find my merchandise. It was bringing in a maximum of three views per day, with no favorites or sales. I regularly get more views by participating in mutual promotion with members of my Etsy team, and that's free!

I would try Search Ads again if Etsy allowed us to specify our own keywords, or they added a pay-per-click system instead of the impression system used now. But word of mouth is more effective, it seems. Paid advertising is not a worthwhile investment for most crafters.

PROTECT YOUR WORK AND MAKE IT LEGAL

Artists, especially those who are starting out, have lots of questions about how to protect their work, how to obey and enforce copyright law and intellectual property. For Etsy crafters, knowing the basics of intellectual property law is important for two major reasons. First, you don't want to unwittingly create and offer for sale something that violates someone else's rights. Secondly, you want to ensure someone else doesn't steal your designs and profit from them.

If you've created something, a design, artwork, or invention from your imagination, you've created intellectual property. Now, how do you prevent someone else from getting rich from your idea? It all depends on what you've created. **Copyright**, for example, can be used to protect something like an original jewelry design, a painting, or writing. A **trademark** may protect a symbol, logo, or made-up word or expression with which you identify your work. If your creation involves a new technology or invention, a **patent** may be the best legal course.

One word of advice, before we get into the minutia: Guard your property, enforce your rights, but don't obsess about this. If you spend most of your time and energy worrying about whether you're not getting credit for something, you've robbed yourself of valuable time you need to develop your business. It's arguably one of the biggest downfalls of new artists and entrepreneurs—they keep their ideas secret, worrying someone will steal them, instead of asking for feedback on their ideas. You'll get a lot further by talking about your ideas with a variety of people, as many people as will listen. That's how you'll know whether you're on the right track—by bouncing your ideas off friends and colleagues, not by bottling them up inside.

As my friend Aaron says: The people who are really capable of "stealing" your idea are usually too busy working on their own things. And the people who **would** rip you off aren't likely to get far anyway. The most important thing, after all, isn't the lightning bolt of inspiration, or a million-in-one invention. It's the passion, the energy, perseverance, commitment, authenticity and obsession to succeed, and working on it day after day. That's how you, and many other people, become successful in business. Nobody gets there simply by stealing ideas.

And besides, imitation is the sincerest form of flattery.

Copyright

Copyright is a protection based on the U.S. Constitution for "original works of authorship" assembled into a tangible medium of expression, such as artwork, books, plays, songs, and architecture. The "medium" might be paper, cloth, ceramics, glass, a computer file, or virtually any other form. As soon as you finish writing, composing, or otherwise assembling such a work, you automatically become the copyright owner, and only you may authorize reproduction and distribution of the work.

Copyright protection exists from the point of creation until 70 years after the death of the creator.

Copyright concerns creative expression and differs from other forms of legal protection such as patents and trademarks. Patents cover inventions, and trademarks protect words and phrases that identify a product or service and distinguish it from competitors.

These three elements, copyright, trademarks and patents, are protections known as "intellectual property" rights.

Derivative works

Sometimes an artist will create a derivative work based on one or more existing copyrighted works. Examples of derivative works are a book translated into a different language, a filmed version of a book, and other adaptations.

Creators of derivative works must obtain permission from the owner of the original copyrights to create the new version.

The key to copyright is that the work must be a creative expression. So copyright doesn't extend to mere facts, ideas, titles, names, slogans, or familiar symbols or designs—although if some of these things were assembled into a new, fixed form of expression, then that could be a copyrighted work.

Copyright doesn't protect standard utilitarian objects like clothing, machines, or household items like dishes. However, such an item may include a copyrighted work—such as a T-shirt that has been enhanced with an original needlepoint design. A plain wooden cigar box can't be copyrighted, but an original carving or painting added to the box's lid could be.

Public domain

When copyright protection expires, works fall into the "public domain."

Public domain works can be used to create derivative works without permission. For example, artwork in the public domain might be repainted or photographed for resale, or freely used as the basis of a new interpretive work.

Concerning U.S. works created after 1977, copyright lasts 70 years after the author's death, then falls into the public domain. But sometimes a work may be restricted under private property laws, even if it's in the public domain. So if you're uncertain of a work's status, ask permission.

For more information, consult *The Public Domain: How to Find & Use Copyright-Free Writings, Music, Art & More* by Stephen Fishman.

Registering your copyright

Copyright protection exists the moment you create a work, regardless of whether you register the work with the U.S. Copyright Office. The advantage to registration is that if your work is infringed upon, and you initiate legal proceedings and prove your case in court, you could collect statutory damages and attorney's fees. If you delay filing copyright longer than three months after publication, however, you'd have to prove the actual damages in court, which can be time-consuming and difficult.

So, it's prudent to register your copyright within three months of creation. Registration is relatively simple and costs $35 through the U.S. Copyright website, Copyright.gov.

You'll receive a registration certificate in the mail within a few months, and the registration creates a public record. But you can immediately place a copyright notice on your work, even if you didn't register. A notice is usually recorded with the word "copyright" or the symbol "©" followed by your name and the year of publication.

Sometimes a work's "author" doesn't own the copyright because they composed the work as part of their job, known in legal parlance as "work for hire."

Licensing your work

Copyright owners may decide it's in their best interest to license their copyrighted work. In this case, the creator would grant someone permission to reproduce the work according to an agreed fee schedule (if any) and duration.

Licensing your works, or selling a copy of a work to an Etsy buyer, doesn't mean you're surrendering a copyright. Unless you've agreed otherwise, selling one of your items only involves the transfer of the physical object, not the intellectual property rights. For example, if you sell an engraved plate, you're only selling the plate. You're not transferring ownership of the design you engraved or the rights to copy it without your permission.

Sometimes Etsy sellers can earn more money by licensing their designs than they can earn by selling items they've handcrafted themselves. For more information, consult *Licensing Art and Design: A Professional's Guide to Licensing and Royalty Agreements* by Caryn R. Leland and *Licensing Art 101: Publishing and Licensing Your Artwork for Profit* by Michael Woodward.

First-sale doctrine and 'fair use' defense

Buyers of a U.S. copyrighted work obtain limited rights from the "first sale doctrine," which allows them to resell the physical object without permission of the copyright owner. For example, if you've purchased a book or a music disk, you're allowed to resell or give away the object without permission of book's author or music's composer. Likewise, if you sell one of your original paintings on Etsy for $20, nothing prevents the buyer from reselling it to their neighbor, or donating the painting to Goodwill. On the other hand, they're not permitted to take a picture of the work and resell or distribute it.

Fair use doctrine allows people to use a portion of a copyrighted work for educational or news usage. For example, book reviews will often quote portions of a book with no special permission from the author. However, if the excerpted work was used for commercial gain—if the excerpted material was resold—a court would probably find the copier guilty of copyright infringement.

One area in some dispute on Etsy is the creation and sale of "fan art," which is artwork based on a character, costume, item, or story created by someone else. For example, an Etsy seller might hand-paint an image onto a coffee mug resembling a movie star. Sometimes the person being depicted (or the creator of the character) would consider such artwork as harmless free advertising—but some would consider it a copyright violation, or an unlicensed product.

The main problem with "fan art" is that many Etsy sellers mistakenly believe that the fair use doctrine protects a seller of such materials, if the seller is actually a "fan" of the person or character being depicted.

"'Fair use' does not protect those who sell the fan art or otherwise make money by using copyrighted work," says Sarah Feingold, Etsy's in-house attorney. If the matter went to court, and the sale of such material wasn't for a recognized nonprofit purpose, the "fan art" creator might be liable for damages, she says. A simple rule bears repeating: If you're in doubt as to whether you have permission to use someone else's imagery, character, or brand, ask.

Likewise, some crafters assume that any materials can be freely upcycled, regardless of whether it contains anyone else's design. Don't bet on it. For example, on any given day, more than a thousand Etsy sellers have upcycled or unlicensed handmade products based on Coca-Cola's logo or containers. There's no way Coke's lawyers can track down every part-time seller who unwittingly violates its trademarks. But anyone who sells much of something shows up on somebody's radar. For example, a few years ago a manufacturer of trendy messenger bags got in hot water for selling "recycled" bags made from used Target shopping bags. Target threatened a lawsuit based on unauthorized use of its logo, and the product quickly disappeared.

Reporting intellectual property theft on Etsy

If you believe another Etsy seller has infringed on your copyright, the first step is to contact them directly and request that the infringement stop. You can also consult an attorney and report the incident to Etsy according to the Etsy Copyright and Intellectual Property Policy, which requires you to put your complaint into writing and mail or fax it to Etsy's office. Once Etsy receives such a complaint and decides it's valid, Etsy may cancel the offending listing, notify the offending seller, and provide details of your complaint, including your email address and other contact information. Copyright violators are subject to account suspension and termination.

Get more information

Further details on copyright law are available at Copyright.gov. For additional facts about patent and trademark law, visit Uspto.gov.

You also can consult Etsy's Copyright and Intellectual Property Policy at Etsy.com/help/article/482.

Selecting a legal form of business

Once you've decided to pursue an Etsy business, you'll need to decide how your business will be formally organized and how you'll meet your tax obligations. As your business grows, you should periodically revisit the question of the best form of organization for your business.

Sole proprietorship. Establishing a sole proprietorship is cheap and relatively simple. This term designates an unincorporated business that is owned by one individual, the simplest form of business organization to start and maintain. You are the sole owner and you take on all the business's liabilities and risks. You state the income and expenses of the business on your own tax return.

Any business that hasn't incorporated is automatically a sole pro-proprietorship. So if you haven't incorporated, formed a partnership, or established a limited liability company, your business is a sole proprietorship by default.

The good news about a sole proprietorship is that you're entitled to all the profits from the business. On the other hand, you are 100 percent responsible for all debts and liabilities. So if your business is sued, your personal assets could be seized.

As a sole proprietorship, you're liable for paying income tax and self-employment tax (Social Security and Medicare taxes), and for filing quarterly estimated taxes based on your net income. Since you don't have an employer reporting your income and withholding a portion of your paycheck for taxes, you must inform the IRS about the income from your Etsy selling and make quarterly tax payments on the profits. Quarterly installments of the estimated tax, submitted with Form 1040-ES, are due April 15, June 15, September 15, and January 15 of the following calendar year. If you don't yet sell full-time and you also work at a job where your employer withholds income for taxes, you can ask your employer to increase your withholding. That way you might avoid having to mail in quarterly estimated payments on your profits.

As far as the IRS is concerned, a sole proprietorship and its owner are treated as a single entity. Business income and losses are reported with your personal tax return on Form 1040, Schedule C, "Profit or Loss From Business."

If you've never filed a Schedule C with the IRS before, you might wish to hire an accountant to assist you with the first year's return. The following year you might complete the return yourself. One helpful tool in this regard is tax-preparation software such as TurboTax or TaxCut. Unlike the IRS instruction pamphlets, these products guide you through the tax-filing process in plain English. The program can save you several hours at tax time because you don't have to decipher the arcane language of the IRS.

- **Partnership.** A partnership is the relationship between two or more persons who agree to operate a business. Each person contributes something toward the business and has a stake in its profits and losses. Partnerships must file an annual information return to report the income and deductions from operations. Instead of paying income tax, the partnership "passes through" profits or losses to the partners, and each partner includes their share of the income or loss on their tax return.

- **Corporation.** In a corporation, prospective shareholders exchange money or property for the corporation's stock. The corporation generally takes deductions similar to those of a sole proprietorship to calculate income and taxes. Corporations may also take special deductions.

- **Limited liability company.** A limited liability company (LLC) is a relatively new business structure allowed by state statute. LLCs are popular because owners have limited personal liability for the company's debts and actions, as is also the case for a corporation.

Local ordinances

Call your county government's headquarters to ask what types of permits and licenses are required for your business. Some cities, counties, and states require any business to get a business license. If you're working at home, your city or county may require a "home occupation permit" or a zoning variance, and you might have to certify that you won't have walk-in retail customers. Since your business is an online and mail-order business, this shouldn't be a problem.

If you are conducting your business under a trade name or your Etsy shop name, you should file a "fictitious name" certificate with your county or state government office so people who deal with your business can find out who the legal owner is. This is also known as a DBA name (Doing Business As) or an "assumed name" or "fictitious name."

Sales taxes. Although the Internet is a "tax-free zone" in many respects, this does not apply to state sales taxes for goods sold to customers in your state. To pay the tax, you'll need to open an account and obtain a "resale license," known as a resale number or sales tax certificate in some instances.

You don't collect state sales tax on orders shipped outside your state. Internet sales, as well as fax, telephone, and mail-order sales shipped to another state, aren't subject to sales tax unless you have an office or warehouse located there. In some states, shipping and handling fees are not subject to sales tax, but in some they are—you will need to investigate the issue for your home state. This is the way things operate today, but there's no guarantee it will stay this way.

Once you've made the decision that your business is no longer a hobby, obtain a resale certificate from your state tax office. This will relieve you of paying state sales tax on the items you buy for resale, but it will also obligate you to report and pay taxes on the sales you make to customers within your state.

A caveat: State sales tax is an evolving area you'll need to monitor. Because online sales are growing so rapidly, local governments are salivating at the prospect of collecting local sales taxes from online sellers, no matter where the item is shipped. Sooner or later, it's inevitable that sellers will be regulated and taxed more than they are today.

Income taxes. Your form of business determines which income tax return form you have to file. For the vast majority of sellers without employees or a walk-in store, a sole proprietorship makes the most sense. As noted previously, the other most common forms of business are partnerships, corporations, and limited liability companies.

Many beginning sellers spend lots of time dreaming about what they'll be able to "write off" on their tax return, now that they have a business. Actually, what you're doing is paying taxes on your net profits. Your write-offs are the costs of doing business, such as buying inventory and paying for postage. What's left over is the profit, and you pay income tax on that.

As far as the IRS is concerned, your business must become profitable within three years or it will be considered a hobby, and none of the expenses will be deductible. For example, your mileage traveling to fairs or the Post Office is deductible for tax purposes. But don't rely on your memory to keep track of such expenses. Keep a notebook in your car to document the mileage and expenses for your buying trips. If you're ever audited, the IRS will want to see documentation for your travel and other deducted expenses.

To figure your taxes, you'll need to keep track of every penny involving your business. Keep receipts and records, and put your expenses into categories such as "postage," "shipping supplies," "inventory," and so on. Your costs for materials, shipping expenses, selling expenses, advertising, mileage and other expenses related to your business are deductible.

Your bookkeeping chores can be greatly simplified with financial software such as Quicken. Most banks offer free downloads of your transactions, and once you set it up, Quicken can automatically categorize all your business expenses and eliminate most of the headaches at tax time. If you have a debit or check card linked to your account, you can use the card for nearly all your business transactions. Those records can be downloaded into Quicken right along with your banking records, making your bookkeeping that much simpler.

If you're familiar with bookkeeping and accounting principles, you might be able to do a better job with QuickBooks software, which is designed especially for small-business accounting.

Another handy tool for keep track of your business income and expenses is Min.com. Its free service enables you to download, categorize, and record transactions from most financial institutions and credit-card accounts.

Supporting documents. The law doesn't require any particular record-keeping technique, as long as you can plainly show your income and expenses. Your records must summarize your business transactions, showing your gross income, deductions, and credits. It's a good idea to have a separate checking account for your business so your personal funds are not included.

You should preserve the paper trail of any purchases, sales, and other transactions, including any invoices or receipts, sales slips, bills, deposit slips, and records of canceled checks. Keep documents that support your tax return organized and in a secure place. More detailed information is available in IRS Publication 583, "Starting a Business and Keeping Records," which is available here: Irs.govpublications/p583/index.html.

In the event you pay more than $600 to someone for services or rent during a calendar year—say, your accountant or a marketing consultant, you're supposed to send that person an IRS 1099 form. For more information, visit Irs.gov/instructions/i1099msc/ar02.html.

Reporting by online marketplaces. Starting in 2011, online payment processors, including PayPal, began providing sellers and the Internal Revenue Service with a summary of their selling activity, which is detailed on an IRS Form 1099-K. The objective was to require online sellers to report their business income and pay any required taxes.

The reporting began with transactions occurring on or after Jan. 1, 2011. It's the result of new IRS regulations that require online marketplaces to generate the forms for sellers with more than 200 transactions and $20,000 in sales during the year.

Your Form 1099-Ks will show a consolidated report of all payments received from your sales. This information is also reported as gross income to the IRS.

The new rules apply to everyone, including part-time sellers and those with more than one small account. For sellers with multiple accounts, the marketplaces combine all of them to calculate your volume status. For example, sellers close to or exceeding the IRS thresholds by the end of the 2011 calendar year would receive 1099-Ks in early 2012.

Business use of your home. You may be able to deduct expenses related to the business use of parts of your home. This deduction is subject to certain requirements and doesn't include expenses such as mortgage interest and real estate taxes.

To qualify to claim expenses for business use of your home, you must use part of your home "exclusively" and regularly as your principal place of business or for storage. This means the area used for your business must be a

room or other separate identifiable space, but you are not required to designate the space by a permanent wall or partition.

There are some exceptions to the "exclusive use" test. If you use part of
your home for storage of inventory, you can claim expenses for the business
use of your home without meeting the exclusive use test — but you must meet
these criteria:

- You keep the inventory in your home for use in your business.

- Your home is your business's only fixed location.

- You use the storage space on a regular basis.

- The space used for storage is a separately identifiable space suitable
for storage.

To qualify under the "regular use" test, you must use a specific area of your
home for business on a regular basis. Incidental or occasional business use is
not regular use as far as the IRS is concerned.

Keeping your books

For a small Etsy business, simple "cash basis" bookkeeping should suffice.
The cash method entails recording income when money is received and expenses as they are paid. "Cash basis" does not necessarily mean your
transactions are in cash, but refers to checks, money orders, and electronic
payments as well as currency. If you're not familiar with the basics of bookkeeping, read *Small Time Operator: How to Start Your Own Business, Keep
Your Books, Pay Your Taxes and Stay Out of Trouble* by Bernard Kamoroff.

Cash accounting is simpler to understand and use than the other type of
bookkeeping, accrual accounting. Businesses are allowed to use cash accounting if annual sales are below $1 million.

Hiring employees. The decision to begin hiring employees is a big step
for any business. Although employees can enable you to expand your selling
and profits, hiring will add tremendously to your paperwork and the extent to
which your business is regulated by the government. Having employees
means that you need to keep payroll records and withhold income, Social
Security, and state taxes, as well as Medicare and worker's compensation insurance. The states and the IRS require timely payroll tax returns and strict
observance of employment laws. Penalties are usually swift and severe for
failure to pay payroll taxes.

An Etsy seller struggling with a busy workload might be tempted to pay
cash "under the table" for help instead of actually hiring employees during

their transition from a one-person shop to employer status. Don't do it. There is no gray area here—such practices are illegal because payroll taxes and worker's compensation insurance aren't being paid.

An alternative to taking on employees is to hire independent outside contractors. You can hire contractors as needed, and the practice entails less paperwork and none of the headaches of paying employment taxes or producing payroll tax returns.

If you hire an independent contractor, make certain the person doing the work understands completely that they are not an employee. Numerous small-business owners have gotten into scrapes with state and federal regulators when their independent contractors were later denied unemployment compensation or were found not to have paid their own Social Security taxes. Also, be aware that the IRS has been tightening its rules on which types of workers can be considered independent contractors.

Insuring your business

You can purchase insurance coverage for any risk your business might expose you to. Discuss this with your insurance agent or consult an insurance broker in your local phone directory for advice on the type of policy that best fits your business.

General liability insurance. General liability insurance covers legal exposure caused by accident, injuries and claims of negligence. Such policies cover payments resulting from bodily injury, property damage, medical expenses, libel, slander, the cost of defending lawsuits, and settlement bonds or judgments required during an appeal procedure.

Product liability insurance. Companies that manufacture, wholesale, distribute, and retail a product may be liable for its safety. Product liability insurance protects against financial loss resulting from defective products that cause injury or bodily harm. The amount of insurance required depends on the products sold or made. For example, a clothing maker faces less risk than a seller of electrical appliances.

Commercial property insurance. Property insurance covers everything related to the loss and damage of company property due to fire, smoke, wind and hail storms, civil disobedience, and vandalism. The definition of "property" can include lost income, business interruption, buildings, computers, company papers, and money.

Home-based business insurance. Contrary to conventional wisdom, regular homeowners' insurance policies rarely cover losses resulting from home-based businesses. Depending on risks to your business, you may add "riders" to your homeowners' policy to cover normal business risks such as property damage. But homeowners' policies only go so far in covering home-based businesses, and you may need to purchase additional policies to cover other risks, such as general and professional liability. For example, some Etsy sellers have experienced difficulty in obtaining insurance coverage for manufacturing baby products.

SELLER PROFILE: Eclectic Skeptic

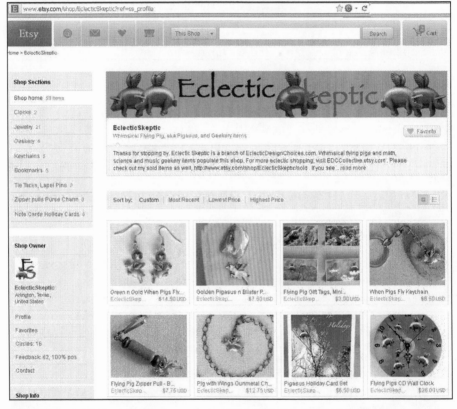

Cathy Stein of Arlington, Texas, sells jewelry and other handcrafted items in the image of whimsical flying pigs, and math, science, and music geekery items. See **Etsy.com/shop/eclecticskeptic**.

How did you get started?

My mom encouraged me to make some jewelry items for a space that she rented in an antique and craft mall. She and I had designed a necklace for a pendant that my husband gave to me. She sold some of my pieces, and I was hooked.

How has your business evolved since you started, and how have you managed during the tough economy?

I started creating just as the economy was headed south. Luckily I went into this endeavor as a part-time business. So while my sales have not been quite what I had hoped, I've not really encountered a hardship because of the economic climate.

The downturn in the economy did cause my mom to close up her space at the mall, and we opened an Etsy shop for my creations and her vintage items at EDCCollective.etsy.com. I opened a second Etsy shop of my own exclusively to sell flying pig items, www.EclecticSkeptic.etsy.com.

My mom passed away during our first holiday shopping season, and now EDCCollective has fewer vintage items, but has branched out into additional handmade items and EclecticSkeptic has added some geekery items for the math, music, and science geek. I have also begun to sell at some local craft shows so that people can see my work in person, and hopefully help build my client base.

What's your creative process?

I love working with cultured freshwater pearls. I especially enjoy using naturally colored pearls in white, cream, peach, and lavender. I often pair pearls with crystal, gemstones, coral, metal, and glass beads. Unless I have a custom request that I need to find specific materials for, I enjoy picking up what "speaks to me" when I go to market. I find that something else that I already have or will trip across shortly will be a perfect fit for it.

The process for my photographic art and wood items is similar. When an image or piece of wood inspires me and matches a project that I have in mind, everything flows from that.

How do you attract customers and get repeat business?

A lot of my online business comes from first-time visitors to Etsy that have found me through Google or Etsy searches. I continually keep an eye out for how I can tweak my listings from an SEO standpoint, to increase my chances of being discovered by people searching for my kind of work.

I also maintain a blog, Eclecticdesignchoices.blogspot.com, a Facebook fan page, and a newsletter to connect to customers. When I sell in person at craft shows, I try to create eye-catching and appealing ways to display my work.

When Pigs Fly Earrings - Red n Silver

Pewter flying pigs fly beneath a column of silver plated and faceted red glass beads. The beads and flying pigs dangle about 1 1/4 inches from the loop of the silver plated ear wires. The red beads sport a flashy AB coating on half of the bead surface.

More flying pig jewelry and other items can be found in my shop, http://www.etsy.com /shop/EclecticSkeptic .

How are your trends regarding online sales and shows?

My goal is to sell more online, and bolster those sales with sales at craft shows. I have a much busier craft show schedule this year than previously.

What is your procedure for pricing your items?

I calculate the cost of my materials and include a profit margin on those, as well as including the cost of my time to create the item. My hourly rate varies slightly depending on the complexity of what I am doing.

STAYING CURRENT WITH ETSY

The Etsy community is a dynamic, organic, sharing community offering virtually unlimited resources of information for advancing your craft and business. For updates to this book and other Etsy news, check my Facebook page: **www.Facebook.com/Etsy101**

The following resources are sponsored by Etsy itself:

Email newsletters

Visit this address to subscribe to these free publications: Etsy.com/mailinglist.

Newsletters		Frequency
Etsy News	Important Admin announcements, site news and upcoming events.	Monthly
Etsy Teams	Opportunities and news in the Etsy Teams community.	Weekly
Etsy Success	Tips from Etsy and top sellers on how to help your shop bloom.	Twice a week
Etsy Labs	Crafty projects and events from the Etsy Labs in Brooklyn.	Weekly
Etsy Finds.	A daily shopping guide to Etsy:	Daily
Etsy Gifts	Gift ideas for everyone on your list.	Seasonally
Etsy Fashion	The hottest style trends on Etsy.	Twice a week
Etsy Weddings	Handmade and vintage picks for brides, grooms, anyone into weddings.	Weekly
Etsy Dudes	Gadgets, gear, fashion and accessories — just for guys.	Weekly

Etsy Help

An online encyclopedia of Etsy information you can navigate by browsing sections or searching for keywords. See Etsy.com/help

Online Labs

Live workshops, and archived videos of previous workshops:

Etsy.com/community/online-labs

Etsy's Facebook page

On the popular social-networking site:

Facebook.com/Etsy

Etsy's Twitter page

Brief announcements and links to new information:

http://twitter.com/etsy

Forums

A multitude of discussion threads focused on Etsy news, announcements, site help, business topics, ideas, and bugs.

Etsy.com/forums.

Etsy Success Team

Here's a team forum geared towards making your shop a success:

Etsy.com/teams/5002/etsy-success

Seller Apps

Tools made by outside developers to help you manage your shop:

Etsy.com/your/apps?show_panel=true

Etsy critique teams

Forums for getting advice about your shop:

Etsy.com/teams/search/critiques

SELLER PROFILE: Jenna's Red Rhino

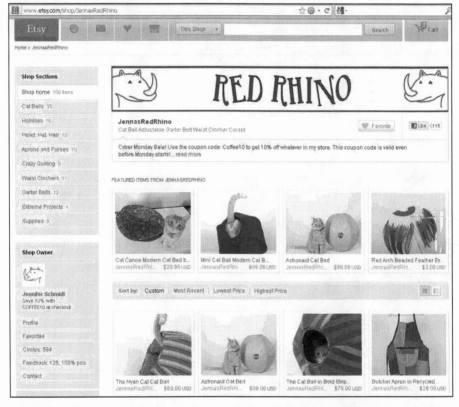

Jennifer Schmidt of Kent, Wash., is an experienced costume designer who began selling custom lingerie, garter belts, and waist cinchers on Etsy.com. Recently Jennifer invented a cat toy and is selling it at her Etsy shop, too. See **Etsy.com/shop/jennasredrhino**.

How did you get started?

I started exploring Etsy as a seller in 2010, while working full-time as a costume designer. I lost my position in costume design in 2011, and decided to go into the handmade business.

One of the things I've noticed in the Etsy marketplace is that the merchandise frequently looks *so* handmade. There are so many repetitive items, tired themes, and work that is not skillfully created. I have high-level sewing and pattern-making skills, and I've been able to create really unique product that is expertly hand-manufactured in my home studio.

The items I'm selling are all my original design, as I make the patterns myself. I use recycled materials where possible, and have developed some items specifically to utilize recycled materials.

How do you get your ideas?

My new ideas usually come from observations and a need to solve problems. For example, I started to design lingerie in response to the specific needs that exotic dancers had for their costuming. They need durable, pretty costumes that also hide figure flaws.

I developed a toy, my Cat Ball, after making careful observations of cat behavior. I knew this item would appeal to cats' instincts and that humans would be entertained watching the cats using it. Even people who do not have cats recognize the appeal.

I am still making custom lingerie, garter belts and waist cinchers, and now I'm also working on wholesale orders for the Cat Ball and have opened an online retail store for this product.

How do you find customers and get repeat business?

My customers find me because of good tagging, stellar photography, unique and humorous product, excellent feedback, photos that demonstrate finishing details, funny stories, and reviews from other sources.

When I sell a Cat Ball, I try to get the cat's name and mention it when sending a shipping notice. If buyers send a photo, then I post this on my website. I try to keep everything about the Cat Bal in a humorous tone, writing funny descriptions, and providing all sorts of silliness on my website.

What retail channels work for you?

So far almost all of my sales have been online, but I've just signed up to be a vendor at an upcoming cat show. So the garter belts are staying home on this trip. I am also preparing the Cat Ball™ for wholesale, as I have been approached a few times with wholesale inquiries.

How do you approach pricing?

Pricing is difficult! I've created spreadsheets that allow me to manipulate variables such as the price of fabric per yard, and these tools are useful. I also compare prices of similar items, but that is difficult for several reasons.

The Jumbo Cat Ball a Unique Cat Bed your Cat Will Love in Carmine Red and Flowers

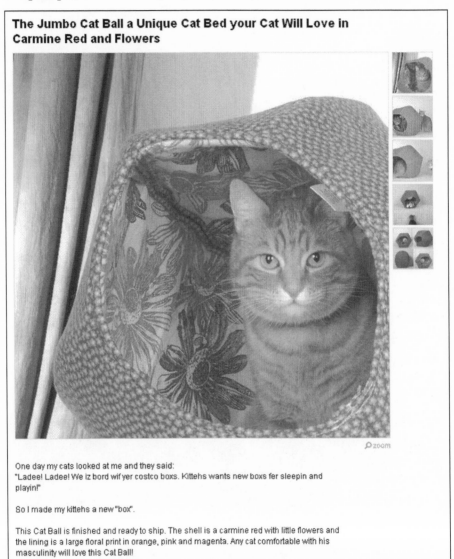

Ω zoom

One day my cats looked at me and they said:
"Ladee! Ladee! We iz bord wif yer costco boxs. Kittehs wants new boxs fer sleepin and playin!"

So I made my kittehs a new "box".

This Cat Ball is finished and ready to ship. The shell is a carmine red with little flowers and the lining is a large floral print in orange, pink and magenta. Any cat comfortable with his masculinity will love this Cat Ball!

In the case of my lingerie, I have difficulty finding anything that I can confirm is as well-made as mine. Other sellers often lack photos that demonstrate the finishing details. Sometimes I can tell from a few photos that the item is of a lesser quality than mine is. In the case of the Cat Ball™, well, it's unique in the marketplace.

Another pricing factor I consider is: How much would I want to pay for it? Ultimately my pricing is a combination of product research, the math, and a gut feeling.

MIND YOUR MANNERS AND DOs & DON'Ts

Etsy is a community. Think of it like the neighborhood where you live. It's smart to behave yourself, give other members the benefit of the doubt, and sometimes hold your tongue, even if you feel like lashing out. Just as you're held responsible for your speech and writing in your neighborhood, you're responsible for acting civilly on Etsy, and for the content submitted through your account. Abide by the site's Terms of Use, which you commit yourself to by joining the site. If you don't comply with the policies, your account can be suspended or terminated.

To clarify, this section is a summary of official Etsy company policy known as "Etsy's Do's and Don'ts." It's not an optional etiquette code that you can choose to follow or ignore. You agree to abide by these rules when you sign up. If you've read this far, these rules should make sense. For reference, the entire, official Etsy list of Do's and Don'ts, which gets quite repetitive, is posted here: Etsy.com/dosdonts.php.

Here's the short course:

• Etsy prohibits the airing of disputes with other parties on its website. Etsy will not mediate disputes, so you'll need to resolve any disagreements with the other party.

• Don't use a trademarked name or the word Etsy in your user name without the company's permission.

• You must be 18 years old to have an Etsy account or have permission from an adult who agrees to supervise the account. Users under 18 are prohibited from using Etsy's community features, such as forums, chat rooms, and virtual labs.

• Language or images considered by Etsy's management to be "profane" or "racist" are prohibited.

• You cannot transfer your Etsy account or sell it to another party.

• Don't use Etsy to send customers to another selling venue to purchase items you have for sale as Etsy—the company considers this "fee avoidance." Accordingly, links and other information about alternate sales venues are verboten.

• Operating more than one account on Etsy is discouraged because of the potential for confusion. If you do operate more than one account, you must disclose it in your public profile for each account, including any accounts you might reserve for buying or selling, and "collective" shops used to sell items from multiple persons. The company won't transfer information such as listings, feedback, favorites, or purchase histories between accounts.

• "Shilling," or using an account you operate to purchase items from yourself, is prohibited.

• You can't list the same unique item in multiple Etsy shops.

• "Collective" shops are permitted in cases of multiple artisans or family members producing handmade items, or business associates who cooperatively manage the account. However, an Etsy collective can't be a group of artists under contract, such as an art agency, gallery, or consignment shop.

• The Public Profile page for all your accounts must specify each person participating in the account, their role in the shop, and the relationships between each participant.

• If you register an Etsy account, you're responsible for its bill and costs of all transactions. If your account is terminated by Etsy, you're still responsible for unpaid fees.

• Etsy "Conversations," also called "Convos," are intended to be used primarily to communicate privately with other Etsy members about a transaction. You can use Convos to build relationships, ask for advice, or discuss Etsy Team activities, but if you suddenly send a large number of messages, this feature might be automatically disabled, and you'll need to contact Etsy's support staff to reset your privilege to send Convos.

• Don't use Convos for unsolicited advertising, harassment, donation requests, or to discourage people from transacting with other members.

• Don't contact Etsy regarding transactions as a first resort. Questions should be directed to the seller, not Etsy, which is merely a platform connecting buyers and sellers. Correspondence should be handled privately through Etsy Convos and email, not on public areas of the site. In cases where you can't resolve a dispute after contacting a member privately, contact Etsy Support for assistance with a transaction.

• Sellers must ship items as described within a reasonable time frame, according to their shop policies, to the address submitted by the buyer. Sellers should keep records of their shipments because in case of a dispute, Etsy may ask sellers to provide proof of shipping. However, Etsy does not hold sellers responsible for delays caused by the Postal Service or other carrier, theft, or customs delays. Likewise, buyers returning an item to the seller aren't held responsible for such mishaps.

• Buyers must pay the seller at the time of the transaction, according to the terms set in the seller's shop policies, and provide valid shipping, payment and billing information. If the buyer does not pay, the seller may cancel the transaction.

• Sellers are prohibited from canceling transactions in order to avoid feedback or fees.

• When sellers fail to ship an item after receiving payment, the buyer may file a non-delivery report with Etsy. In such cases, the buyer and seller receive a notice from Etsy with instructions on resolving the transaction. Buyers and sellers must respond to non-delivery notices or face account suspension or termination.

• In certain cases, sellers may refuse service to a buyer before shipment, and notify the buyer via email or Etsy Convos. If the buyer has paid, sellers must refund the item price and shipping fee. Members who, in Etsy's judgment, "abuse" the right to refuse service are subject to account suspension or termination.

• Sellers must accurately describe their items. If a buyer receives something "significantly" different from the listing, they may report the discrepancy, "item not as described," to Etsy support.

• Don't engage in "transaction interference," which includes communicating with Etsy members to "warn" them of a particular item, buyer, or seller.

• In the event of canceled or voided transactions, Etsy issues a refund for the applicable fees, and removes the transaction. Only sellers may cancel a transaction. Buyers requesting cancellation should contact the seller, and in the event of no response, contact Etsy Support.

- Returns of items are subject to the seller's shop policies, and buyers must contact sellers for approval before returning an item.

- Sellers may cancel or void transactions in these cases: (1) After shipment, in the event the buyer doesn't receive the item, and the seller refunds the price paid for the item; and (2) Buyer and seller agree the buyer may return an item for a refund, and the seller has refunded the item price paid.

- When submitting feedback, don't include personally identifying, private information such as a real name, phone number, street or email address, content of Etsy Convos, or details of Etsy investigations.

- Don't include in your feedback any mature, racist, or profane language or images, or any links or advertising.

- Don't offer for sale mass-produced items in Etsy's "handmade" category. Don't try to pass off as "handmade" something from a "ready to assemble" kit unless you've substantially altered the original design. Handmade items may include vintage items that have been upcycled, reconstructed or significantly altered.

- Reselling is prohibited. You can't list handmade items that weren't created by you or a shop member.

- Don't list a gift basket in Etsy's handmade category if it consists solely of repackaged mass-produced items.

- Third-party vendors may be used to assist in the creation of handmade items in the following types of cases: printing or reproducing artwork originated by the seller, casting metal from the seller's mold, or kiln-firing ceramics from the seller's work. If you have someone assisting you with the creative process or administrative tasks such as shipping items or communicating with buyers, the person must be under your direct supervision. Assistants or vendors can't comprise a majority share of the creation of handmade items.

- Don't list services for sale on Etsy, except those that produce a product. For example, restoring, tailoring, or repair services aren't allowed. The creation of custom products and designs, including digital files, is allowed.

• Sellers may offer instructional workshops only if they provide the buyer with a tangible product, like a manual, craft supplies, or a project the student works on.

• Don't list for sale in Etsy's "Commercial Crafting Supply" category items that are finished products, such as clothing or dollhouse furniture.

• Commercial tools and accessories intended for use with a handmade item, such as a makeup brush, can't be listed in Etsy's commercial crafting supply category.

• Don't list an item as "vintage" unless it's at least 20 years old.

• Items that have been reconstructed, upcycled, or significantly altered are prohibited in Etsy's Vintage category, but can qualify for the handmade category.

• Unaltered, repaired, or restored items are permitted in the Vintage category.

• Don't advertise or engage in charitable fundraising via Etsy unless you understand and comply with the several laws governing these activities, in addition to Etsy's special requirements for fundraising listings. Don't create listings solely to solicit donations.

• If you use "mature" content on Etsy such as depictions of genitalia, sexual themes, or violent or profane language, such content must be tagged "mature" and you must include the word "mature" in the item's listing title. Mature content can't be used within Etsy user names, item titles, avatars, profiles, shop announcements, or titles of shop sections.

• Don't include mature content in the first thumbnail image of your listing.

• Don't list for sale the following items, which are prohibited by Etsy:

1. Alcohol

2. Tobacco

3. Drugs, drug-like substances, drug paraphernalia

4. Live animals, illegal animal products

5. Pornography

6. Firearms and/or weapons

7. Recalled items

8. Real estate

9. Motor vehicles (automobiles, motorcycles, boats, etc.)

10. Items or listings that promote, support or glorify hatred toward or otherwise demean people based upon: race, ethnicity, religion, gender, gender identity, disability, or sexual orientation; including items or content that promote organizations with such views

11. Items or listings that promote or support illegal activity or instruct others to engage in illegal activity

12. Items or listings that promote, support or glorify acts of violence or harm towards self or others

• Don't specify a "minimum" purchase amount in your Etsy shop, which is prohibited.

• Make your Etsy listings clear, detailed, and accurate. Correct, representative photos and accurate descriptions and listing information are essential.

• Ensure that each listing you have is actually available for purchase and prompt shipping.

• Don't create listings for items that are sold out.

• Don't create listings merely to share photographs or information with Etsy members.

• Listings that are merely advertisements are prohibited, including notices of sales or promotions in your shop. You may, however, include such information in your shop announcements, profile, avatar, banner and item descriptions.

• Don't offer items for rent or leasing, which is prohibited on Etsy.

• You must list your item at a "reasonable" price, and not with an artificially high price intended to discourage purchases.

• Don't pad your shipping fee. Etsy requires shipping fees to be "reasonable."

• Create a separate listing for each unique item. Group items into a single listing only if they're being sold and shipped together as a set.

- Don't edit an existing listing in order to change it to a different item, a practice Etsy considers "fee avoidance."

- Don't offer items conditionally—you can't require additional purchases of other listings in your shop, even for item upgrades, gift-wrapping, or shipping discounts.

- You may offer additional "free with purchase" items, but the offer may be mentioned only in the item description, not item titles, tags, or photographs.

- If you offer gift certificates on Etsy, you must comply with local laws, which may vary. Your listing for gift certificates must include the statement, "This Gift Certificate is valid only in my Etsy shop, and it is only redeemable here."

- "Drop shipping" is prohibited on Etsy. In other words, you must have all listed item on hand, available for prompt shipping under your direct supervision.

- Label your listings only with words that accurately describe the item. Synonyms are OK (describing a purse as a "handbag") but labels that don't directly apply (describing earrings as a "necklace") is against policy.

- If the item you're offering is a reproduction or an edition of multiples, don't describe it as "original," "one of a kind," "OOAK."

- Tags may be a short, accurate phrase, such as "stainless steel" or "reversible jacket," but you can't use multiple words that aren't a phrase, such as "red purple blue."

- Tags can't refer to potential uses for your item. For example, don't label beads as a "necklace."

- Tags related to the crafting or assembly of an item, such as "woodworking," can be used only to refer to the procedure that you personally employed to create the item.

- Use the flagging procedure, the "Report this item to Etsy" link, to notify the company of listings that violate Etsy policy. Don't flag the same listing multiple times.

- Don't flag Etsy listings in cases of suspected intellectual property issues. Instead, follow the "Copyright and Intellectual Property Policy."

- Keep a positive, constructive attitude on Etsy's community areas. Berating, insulting, or harassing other members is prohibited.

- Don't post unsolicited advertising, or spam, in Etsy's forums or other public areas. Don't promote outside websites, services, or products.

- Keep forum posts on-topic and constructive.

- Don't use Etsy teams to discuss or demonstrate disputes with other members.

- Don't use the word "Etsy" or other trademarked terms in your team name.

- Don't use Etsy's Treasury feature to list or comment on a listing or member in a negative light.

When you sign up for Etsy, you agree to the following:

1. The content you post is not false, inaccurate or misleading

2. You won't commit fraud or sell illegal, counterfeit or stolen items

3. You won't infringe upon any third party's copyright, patent, trademark, trade secret, or other proprietary or intellectual property rights or rights of publicity or privacy.

4. You won't sell items that have been identified by the U.S. Consumer Products Safety Commission (CPSC) as hazardous to consumers and therefore subject to a recall

5. You won't be defamatory, trade libelous, unlawfully threatening, unlawfully harassing, impersonate or intimidate any person (including Etsy staff or other users), or falsely state or otherwise misrepresent your affiliation with any person, through, for example, the use of similar email address, nicknames, or creation of false account(s) or any other method or device

6. You won't be obscene or possess child pornography

7. Your listings will not contain or transmit any code of a destructive nature that may damage, detrimentally interfere with, surreptitiously intercept or expropriate any system, data or personal information

8. You won't modify, adapt or hack Etsy or modify another website so as to falsely imply that it is associated with Etsy;

9. You won't appear to create liability for Etsy or cause Etsy to lose (in whole or in part) the services of Etsy's ISPs or other suppliers

- ETSY, and other Etsy graphics, logos, designs, page headers, button icons, scripts, and service names are registered trademarks in the U.S. and/or other countries. Etsy's trademarks may not be used, including as part of trademarks and/or as part of domain names or email addresses, in connection with any product or service in any manner that is likely to cause confusion.

SELLER PROFILE: Custom Hemp Treasures

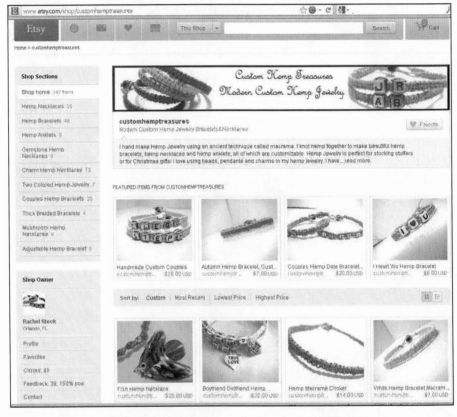

Rachel Steck of Orlando, Fla., has been crafting since high school days, and is busy with two Etsy shops. One offers custom handmade hemp jewelry; the other her hand-knit scarves and beanies. See **Etsy.com/shop/CustomHempTreasures** and **Etsy.com/shop/CustomKnitTreasures**.

How did you get started?

I started making handmade hemp jewelry in high school. One day I wore a necklace to school, and everyone wanted one! So I started selling them to my friends.

I also started knitting in high school after my mom taught me. It took many years to perfect my crafts and start selling online.

How has business progressed?

My hemp business started off very slow and simplistic. Over the years I've gotten more business, more customers, and my designs and techniques have evolved.

Eco-friendly items are a trend in general, but to me it's always been just a part of life.

My knitting business took off faster, and I had more orders to start off with. But since those items have more of a seasonal nature, they sell faster in the fall and winter.

Yellow Hemp Bracelet Spiral Knot

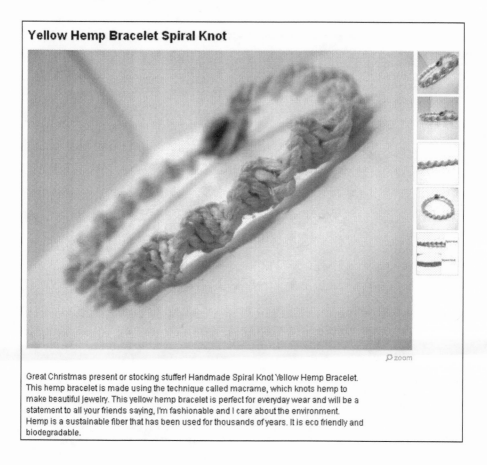

зoom

Great Christmas present or stocking stuffer! Handmade Spiral Knot Yellow Hemp Bracelet. This hemp bracelet is made using the technique called macrame, which knots hemp to make beautiful jewelry. This yellow hemp bracelet is perfect for everyday wear and will be a statement to all your friends saying, I'm fashionable and I care about the environment. Hemp is a sustainable fiber that has been used for thousands of years. It is eco friendly and biodegradable.

Where do your ideas come from?

Everyday life. One day I was driving down the street and I saw a cow in a field. It inspired my Cow Hemp Bracelet. I also love going to craft stores, like Jo-Ann's and Michael's, and just looking at beads. It inspires me to create new items.

Where do you get customers and repeat business?

Both of my businesses are based on Etsy, which has millions of active buyers and sellers. Hemp jewelry is unique and a fairly niche market, so online selling works well for me. I offer a modern, fashionable selection, as well as the traditional hippie-inspired hemp jewelry, with mushroom pendants and such. I get repeat buyers because of my high quality and unique products, and my feedback is 100 percent positive.

What percentage of your business is online vs. offline?

My percentage of business from online is about 99 percent. I sell a few pieces to neighbors and friends, but the majority of my time is spent selling online. I have tried farmers markets, but realized it isn't the right place for my jewelry.

How do you determine prices?

My pricing model for my hemp jewelry has remained nearly the same over the years. I charge a flat rate for simple hemp jewelry with tan hemp and no beads or embellishments. I add $1 for colored hemp on bracelets, and $2 for colored hemp on necklaces. Then I add the cost of any added beads, charms, or pendants.

For my scarves, it takes me about 24 hours to make a 70-inch scarf, and I charge $60.

Index

Made in the USA
Lexington, KY
16 May 2012